Praying Through First John

Volume 1

Scale the Heights of God's Love!

Praying Through First John

Volume 1

Scale the Heights of God's Love!

Mary Jane Fischer

Dedication

To God for His gifts; to George, my challenging partner and shining example; to Jeff who spoke these challenging words which the Lord has kept before me: "Keep the pipeline flowing;" to my loving family who has supported, believed, and encouraged me at every opportunity; to my friend Jeannie who has listened to me for hours and has given many constructive helps; to my deceased mentor, Irene, who challenged me repeatedly with the scripture, "To whom much is given, from him much will be required" (Luke 12:48). To all of these I express gratitude.

Contents

Chapter Two

Chapter Three

Chapter Four

Chapter Five

Dear Fellow Mountain Climber,

I'm a pilgrim on an exciting journey to go forward with God. I do not take this journey alone. I believe we journey together, each one strengthening the other, for it is in this give and take that we grow in Christlikeness.

It is my strong conviction that we Christians haven't even begun to tap the resources God has provided for us to live this glorious Christian life! He wants a growing, intimate relationship with every believer. This relationship is developed and strengthened through meditation and prayer. These are the keys that open our understanding of ourselves and of God. Praying His Word back to Him is a glorious privilege and a powerful experience some have yet to experience!

Through sincere and honest conversations with God we learn more about ourselves and gain a better understanding of God's personal message to us. I believe God reveals more and more of Himself as we're willing to listen to and act upon His entire message to us. He wants us to dwell in His Word and take the time to digest what His Spirit is trying to reveal to us. Growth comes as we release ourselves honestly and passionately to God. He wants hungry, seeking people who spend time with Him daily. He wants us to interact with Him through His Word. When we devote the time to these activities, He gives the increase!

Jesus learned obedience through the things He suffered. We practice obedience by passionate, honest sharing of our hearts daily with Him, especially when we pray in response to His total Word. It is not always an easy discipline. Reading God's Word over and over, verse by verse and letting it saturate the heart takes time. Sacrificing this time for God is sometimes difficult. Perhaps before committing to such a discipline, we should ask ourselves, "Am I willing to follow through with this?"

We are on a search—a glorious journey, and we travel together. As fellow believers and members of the body of Christ, my strength is your strength, and your strength is my strength. We give to one another unselfishly and receive graciously. I give you these prayers. May they strengthen your desire to pray openly and honestly on a daily basis. May these prayers help turn *your heart toward a daily desire to meditate in God's Word, to wait upon Him, and to share with others a passionate desire to know Him better. As we do these things, He will give the increase!*

How beautiful on the mountains are the feet of those who bring good news. —Isaiah 52:7 NIV

Chapter One
A Pilgrim's Prayer

*H*eavenly Father, help me find my rest and peace in You today. The world and daily commitments are constantly clamoring for my attention. What confusion there seems to be. Responsibilities abound, and there seems to be no end to the things I must do. Needs are abundant in every area of my life. Lord, speak in the midst of all this clutter and confusion. Let me hear Your direction, and focus my attention upon You. Touch my soul, and let me breathe in Your calming presence.

As I relax before You, I thank You for renewed confidence and vigor, for the certainty that You have a plan and a personal pattern for my life. Thank You for steadying my heart and filling it with peace when the demands of life come toward me from every direction. Lord God, even in moments of great stress, You come in Your mercy and supply relief. Free me from the extra stress I create when I look for the approval of men and strive to please the world rather than You. Let me hear

Your direction, and Yours alone, for when I am led by You there is peace.

Today is another clean slate upon which to begin afresh and anew. Write upon the blank sheet of my day. Give me Your instructions for the day. Help me forego my own desires and give me patience to wait for what You have for me. Come as the wind, and blow Your divine thoughts gently to me, for in Your thoughts are all wisdom, understanding, and peace. Thank You for filling my heart with all that I need to accomplish Your will for my life. In Jesus' name. Amen.

The Word of Life

That which was from the beginning, which we have heard, which we have seen with our eyes, which we have looked upon, and our hands have handled, concerning the Word of life. (1 John 1:1)

*F*ather, as I begin reading this First Epistle of *John*, I am in awe of the wisdom of the author, the apostle John. He wanted it known from the start that this Jesus he was telling us about existed from the beginning of time!

John wanted us to know the *reality* of Jesus' existence, and that He was not only human, but divine. John made it clear that he had walked, talked, and lived with the Messiah, the Savior of the world! John said he heard Him, saw Him, watched Him, and touched Him while He was on the earth.

In this passage, he called Jesus, the "Word of life." How radiant and revealing the title, "The Word of Life" is! It gives credance to John's statement made in His gospel about Jesus, when he said, "In the beginning was the Word and the Word was with God, and the Word was God" (John 1:1). Jesus was God in the flesh!

Thank You, Lord, for Your Word which tells us, "Christ was alive when the world began, yet I myself have seen him with my own eyes and listened to him speak. I have touched him with my own hands. He is God's message of Life" (1 John 1:1 TLB).

Thank You for the privilege of hearing, seeing, and touching You this morning by reading and meditating upon Your Word. Open my understanding more and more as I wait upon You. In Jesus' name. Amen.

Jesus, the Manifested Life

The life was manifested, and we have seen, and bear witness, and declare to you that eternal life which was with the Father and was manifested to us. (1 John 1:2)

Dear God of all life, thank You for coming in bodily, physical form to our earth! Thank You for manifesting Yourself in the form of a man who our eyes might see and our hands might touch.

Open my spiritual eyes this day to see Your manifested life all around me. Help me to see Your joy in others. Help me to see the sunshine of Your love radiating everywhere. Help me feel Your presence throughout my day.

O, God of the universe, thank You for coming in the form of our Savior. Thank You for Jesus, who lived, died, arose, and sent His Holy Spirit as our guide. You give Your assurance that Jesus sits at Your right hand, Father, making intercession for all who believe. My heart bursts with this miraculous, ongoing truth! Let it continue to grow and flow out of me in joy. Let me be a witness for Jesus Christ today. In Jesus' name. Amen.

How beautiful on the mountains are the feet of those who bring good news. —Isaiah 52:7 NIV

Fellowship

That which we have seen and heard we declare to you, that you also may have fellowship with us; and truly our fellowship is with the Father and with His Son Jesus Christ. (1 John 1.3)

Lord God, as I think upon the wonderful word, fellowship, I recall once again, Jesus' words in John 14:20: "At that day you will know that I am in My Father, and you in Me, and I in you." And then again in John 17:21: "that they may all be one, as You, Father, are in Me, and I in You; that they also may be one in Us, that the world may believe that you sent me." Thank You for these words that help me understand the true essence of "fellowship." I rejoice in this fellowship with You, Lord, and desire this for all Christians everywhere. Help me to covet this for others more and more.

And Lord, as You increase my desire to see others know You more, purify my motives so that my declarations resound with the fullness of Your love. Let this love move among all of us today, that we, in the body of Christ, have true fellowship with one another, with You, Jesus, with our Father, and with Your precious Holy Spirit. In Jesus' name. Amen.

How beautiful on the mountains are the feet of those who bring good news. —Isaiah 52:7 NIV

Fullness of Joy

*And these things we write to you that your joy
may be full. (1 John 1:4)*

Lord God, where does love end and joy begin? I love You with all of my heart, soul, and body. I love You with an undying love. Help my love be so constant that joy, pure joy permeates my entire being! Fill me now with Your love, so that I might overflow for Your glory and demonstrate Your love to others.

Help me help others today toward this fullness of joy. There is such serenity in this joy, such peace, such gratitude! And Lord Jesus, as I help others through loving, accepting, and understanding words, let my joy become more full also. What a privilege it is to serve You! Come, Lord Jesus. Take over my life today. In Jesus' name. Amen.

God Is Light!

This is the message which we have heard from Him and declare to you, that God is light and in Him is no darkness at all. (1 John 1:5)

Oh glorious day, when Light came into this world! You came, Lord Jesus, to light up the world, and to bring light to all those who walk in darkness. Your concept of light has many beautiful, diversified meanings, all of them pointing to the wonders of Your glory at work in the world!

I'm remembering the childhood song which left an indelible impression, "This little light of mine, I'm going to let it shine. This little light of mine, I'm going to let it shine. Let it shine, let it shine, let it shine!" And now, Father, you bring to my mind Your words, "Let your light so shine before men, that they may see your good works and glorify your Father in heaven" Mt. 5:16.

Oh glorious day, when that Light shined into my heart—darkness turned to light, and gloom disappeared. You took over, and continue to take over the reins of my heart. Thank You for Your words, "...in Him is no darkness at all." Help me be "in You" today, that I might reflect the light of Your great and gracious love to others. In Jesus' name. Amen.

How beautiful on the mountains are the feet of those who bring good news. —Isaiah 52:7 NIV

Walking in Light

If we say that we have fellowship with Him, and walk in darkness, we lie and do not practice the truth. (1 John 1:6)

Thank You, Lord, for this precious walk with You. Thank You for the awareness of Your presence when I pray. I praise You today, dear Lord. I open my heart anew for Your cleansing. Come in, Lord Jesus, and purge me from sin. I desire to experience that fellowship with You for which I was created.

Help me to walk in Your light throughout this day. Because You created me, You know my weaknesses better than I know them myself. Lord, keep me close to You. Help me to realize that darkness is an available, ever-present danger in the body of Christ. Keep my feet from slipping, as I strive to speak and walk in truth. In Jesus' name. Amen.

The Cleansing Blood

But if we walk in the light as He is in the light, we have fellowship with one another, and the blood of Jesus Christ His Son cleanses us from all sin. (1 John 1:7)

*F*ather God, thank You for Your commandments that lead me into all truth. Thank You for the blessing of Your daily instruction. Your words are life! There is no end to the blessings You will bestow on every child of God who seeks Your face, so help me to daily follow Your will and seek to know You in Your fullness. Seeking You daily is a difficult discipline to maintain at times, so I ask for Your help for I cannot do it in my own strength.

Thank You for Your commandment that I am to walk in the light just as You are in the light. I'm so grateful for Your promise that we all, if we walk in the light, have fellowship with one another, and that the blood of Jesus Christ, Your Son, cleanses us from all sin. Strengthen Christians everywhere today. Help us all to walk in the light of Your presence, for we need the cleansing blood of Jesus Christ every day! I pray in His name. Amen.

How beautiful on the mountains are the feet of those who bring good news. —Isaiah 52:7 NIV

Repentance

If we say that we have no sin, we deceive ourselves, and the truth is not in us. (1 John 1:8)

Thank You, Lord, for this precious time of prayer—this early morning hour when the world can be shut out and I am able to cloister myself away with You. Refreshment comes when I slow down, read Your Word, pray, and listen patiently for Your voice. Help me to be unhurried in my time with You, Lord. Calm my spirit and allow me to relax in Your presence.

Today, Your Word tells me to admit my sinfulness, and so I acknowledge my sins before You. I have many weaknesses which have not yet been crucified. As I think back over the past twenty-four hours, I recall times when I have sinned against You and Your Word. Thank You for Your gentle conviction which leads me to confession and repentance. Forgive my self-centeredness and fill me with new compassion for others. Thank You for Your blood which cleanses me from all unrighteousness! In Jesus' name. Amen.

Truth in Us

If we say we have no sin, we deceive ourselves,
and the truth is not in us. (1 John 1:8)

Lord, Your Word tells us, "If we say we have no sin, we deceive ourselves, and the truth is not in us." In my human condition, I know that I am sinful. So there is a daily need to share my shortcomings with You. It is humbling to bow before You daily in repentance. The Apostle Paul said, "When I try not to do wrong, I do it anyway. . . It is plain where the trouble is: sin still has me in its evil grasp" (Ro. 7:19–20 TLB).

I desire to be honest with You and have Your truth dwell in me. Touch me with Your cleansing power today, and make me clean. Thank You for Your cleansing touch that makes me a worthy vessel to be used by You and for Your purposes. I pray that Your name would be glorified through my actions today. In Jesus' name. Amen.

God Is Faithful and Just

If we confess our sins, He is faithful and just to forgive us our sins and to cleanse us from all unrighteousness. (1 John 1:9)

*L*ord, so little is said and taught in the body of Christ about our need to ask Your forgiveness for sin on a regular basis. Each time I come to You confessing my sins, You lift me anew into that realm of freedom. This exhilarating freedom You give is difficult to explain. This freedom releases Your anointing and opens the flood gates of love, forgiveness and joy!

The apostle Paul said, long after he was first saved by Jesus Christ, "I know that in me (that is, in my flesh) nothing good dwells" (Ro. 7:18). Lord God, teach me anew that if it were not for Your indwelling Spirit and influence, I would be altogether unlovely. Many times I need to be cleansed from old habits, wrong thinking patterns, or my failure to follow Your leadership or to obey things You tell me to do. Thank You for Your faithfulness, Your justice, and Your mercy. Thank You for the great vastness of Your mercy and the gentleness of Your Holy Spirit. In Jesus' name. Amen.

How beautiful on the mountains are the feet of those who bring good news. —Isaiah 52:7 NIV

Making God a Liar

*If we say we have no sin, we make Him a liar,
and His word is not in us. (1 John 1:10)*

John the apostle said, "If we say we have not sinned, we are deceiving ourselves" (1 John 1:8). How well he knew his own framework and the framework of all humankind! How easy it is for me to deny You through daily neglect! How easy it is to make You a liar, Lord Jesus, by failing to praise You, love You, and confess my sins to You. Sometimes I make You, Lord God, a liar simply by not acknowledging my sins or by neglecting my daily prayer time with You.

Lord Jesus, if I deny Your commands, I am denying You. I am also saying, in a sense, "I don't believe Your Word. You are not as good as Your Word." Therefore, I am saying to You, "You lie, and Your word is not truth."

I do not want to make You a liar, O Lord. Instill Your Word in my heart today, that I might not sin against You. Give me the courage to come to You as a little child, in honesty and with true confession. Give me a repentant heart and renew a right spirit within me. How I need this renewal and cleansing each day. Thank You for the ministry of Your Spirit which makes it possible. I love You, Lord, and I praise You with my whole heart! In Jesus' name. Amen.

How beautiful on the mountains are the feet of those who bring good news. —Isaiah 52:7 NIV

A Pilgrim's Prayer

My heart looks up to You this day, Almighty God! So many things I do not understand, but I do understand Your greatness. I understand Your greatness is so big, that I, a mere mortal, will never fully understand the many dimensions of Your love.

You said, "Behold, I stand at the door and knock. If anyone hears My voice and opens the door, I will come in to him and dine with him, and he with Me" (Rev. 3:20). Who am I that You should have time for me? Who am I that You should fellowship with me when I come seeking time with You? You are the great and mighty God!

I come in deep gratitude. I come praising You for reigning supreme in my life. I come acknowledging Your tremendous love which no one will ever fully comprehend or understand. How grateful I am for heavenly fellowship with You as I walk this earth.

Thank You for molding me day by day into the image of Your Son, Jesus. Thank You for the privilege of spending time with You in prayer and in the Word.

Thank You for Your faithfulness to speak to my heart. I open myself to You today, Almighty God. Speak afresh Your affirming love as I praise Your holy name. In Jesus' name. Amen.

How beautiful on the mountains are the feet of those who bring good news. —Isaiah 52:7 NIV

Chapter Two
A Pilgrim's Prayer

My Father and my God, how grateful I am for the privilege of addressing You anytime, anywhere, and in any place or circumstance. Thank You that You are a God of mercy, who is always caring and always listening. Thank You for the vastness of Your mercy. As I contemplate how deep Your love is for me, I am amazed at the breadth and width of Your concern for all mankind!

Grant me a measure of Your mercy, so that I would have the desire and the ability to reach beyond myself and strengthen someone else who needs to feel Your touch—someone who may not know You.

How tempting it is to just nestle down into Your love and only enjoy Your presence just for myself. How easy it is to revel in the truths I understand, but forget those who are searching for truth, waiting to hear the glorious good news about Your love for them.

O God, forgive me for taking Your love for granted. Forgive me for becoming selfish and self-satisfied, only focused on my own needs and desires. Forgive me for being negligent of my time with You when it is at that time that I need, above all else, to seek Your face daily. I need Your truth—Your truth that will prompt me to share Your love with others.

Father, we, as believers, comprise a kingdom of kings and priests. Because we are a part of Your kingdom, we must walk in humility, putting others before ourselves, giving of ourselves, and sacrificing for others. In Your kingdom, those who would be the greatest are the ones who are the most willing to serve.

Forgive me for my own sins, and enable me to intercede for the sins of others. Lord, we as Christians are called to a higher calling because You have set us apart from the world. I now ask You to grant us the willingness to serve unselfishly and charitably for Your sake. In Jesus' name. Amen.

Childlike Faith

My little children, these things I write to you.
(1 John 2:1a)

Father, the apostle John In Your Word addresses me as a little child. In my relationship with You, I want to become more and more as a little child. The Lord Jesus said, "whoever does not receive the Kingdom of God as a little child will by no means enter it" (Luke 18:17). Lord, increase my faith and cause it to become more and more trusting and childlike. I will then believe—without hesitation—that prayer moves mountains, and that You are capable of mighty deeds in my life! By becoming like a child, the truths of Your Word will be better absorbed, retained, and applied every day.

The apostle John loved the body of Christ so dearly that he called us "little children." Lord, open my heart so that I may respond to you in a childlike way. Help me respond to Your call and instructions with childlike faith. Move mountains through my prayers, and let mighty deeds be done in my life! In Jesus' name. Amen.

Our Advocate and Sacrifice

My little children, these things I write to you, so that you may not sin. And if anyone sins, we have an Advocate with the Father, Jesus Christ the righteous. And He Himself is the propitiation for our sins, and not for ours only but also for the whole world. (1 John 2:1,2)

I wait upon You, Lord God. Bless me with Your presence during this time of prayer. I reach out in faith for Your touch. I wait upon You for Your guidance. In Your Word, You admonish me not to sin. I need that reminder, for I am human and have many weaknesses. I need to stand strong against temptation when it comes. What a relief it is to me when You say in Your Word, "And if anyone sins, we have an Advocate with the Father, Jesus Christ the righteous!"

Your love is gentle and kind. Your love allows me to be human, and I thank You for Your mercy. You understand my weaknesses for You, too, Jesus, have been tempted. Thank You for Your Holy Spirit who is present to lead me in the right way. Thank You, also, for Your Holy Spirit who convicts me if I take a wrong turn. I am so grateful for Jesus Christ who sits at Your right side, making intercession for me! In Jesus' name. Amen.

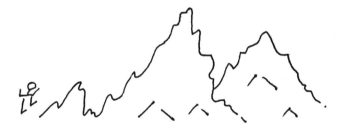

How beautiful on the mountains are the feet of those who bring good news. —Isaiah 52:7 NIV

Knowing God

We know that we have come to know him if we obey his commands. (1 John 2:3 NIV)

Lord God, thank You for a new thirst in our world for spiritual things—for people who are searching for You. Thank You for "hungering and thirsting" hearts that are searching for new meaning in life in a world that becomes more and more chaotic each day. Teach me that I too, must hunger for you and seek daily to know You more.

You tell me in Your Word that to know You is to know Your commandments. How good it is that You have given us a Person, Jesus Christ, after whom we can pattern our lives. And You've given us Your Word which contains all the instructions we need to walk out our Christian faith day by day. Teach me how to conform my will to Your will, and help me to daily seek out your will for my life. In Jesus' name. Amen.

Keeping His Commandments

He who says, "I know Him," and does not keep His commandments, is a liar, and the truth is not in him. (1 John 2:4)

Lord, sometimes Your Word is difficult for us to follow. It isn't difficult to understand; but it is difficult to obey. I know that to know You fully, I must keep Your commandments. And if I don't keep Your commandments, I cannot say I know You. I know that there is no truth in me, and that I am a liar if I don't keep Your commandments. Lord God, I want to always follow Your Word. I want to always be able to say, truthfully, "I know Him!"

Lord, I will work at knowing You through studying Your Word and obeying Your commands. I am sometimes weak and often without discipline. Please help me and give me the daily strength I need to keep Your commandments and progress toward knowing You. I need Your truth inside me. In Your mercy and grace, supply my need for discipline. I want to know You better on a daily basis. Fill me with Your truth, that I might keep Your commandments. In Jesus' name. Amen.

How beautiful on the mountains are the feet of those who bring good news. —Isaiah 52:7 NIV

God's Words Are
His Commandments

But whoever keeps His word, truly the love of God is perfected in him. (1 John 2:5a)

Lord, thank You for Your word that gives me what I need to "keep on keeping on." There seems to be no limit to the new discoveries I find as I know You more and more. But Lord, I do take Your word for granted at times. In my humanness, I ignore it when things are going well, but then return to it when I have needs. Thank You so much for Your faithfulness. You love me so much that when I return to You, You are there waiting for me!

You will never leave me nor forsake me. Your love is constant and Your blessings are plentiful when I seek You in Your Word. You are calling me to obey Your commandments, Your Word. Lead me in Your Word so that I might learn to obey Your instruction. In Jesus' name. Amen.

Walking in Him

> *But whoever keeps His word, truly the love of God is perfected in him. By this we know that we are in Him. (1 John 2:5)*

*J*elp me walk in step with You today, Lord. The more I learn of You, the more I realize how much more I need to learn! I want to be "in You," as Your Word tells me to be, but often I know that I am walking according to my own desires. I have good intentions, but I revert to my own ideas and plans too easily.

Your promise to us is that Your love will be perfected in us as we keep Your word. Forgive me for walking in my own way and for making decisions according to the way I believe things should be. Teach me, as I spend time in Your Word, how to wait upon You and follow Your instructions. Perfect Your love in my heart as I learn to love You more. Teach me, again and again, to walk "in You." In Jesus' name. Amen.

Walk as Jesus Walked

He who says he abides in Him ought himself also to walk just as He walked. (1 John 2:6)

Good morning, Lord! I open Your Word with great assurance, as I know You will meet me during this time spent with You. I come with open hands as Your child, knowing You will fill me with blessing and purpose because I seek fellowship with You. Help my own words that they will be true for Your glory. Touch my ears so that I may be able to hear Your voice and discern Your will.

I abide in You, but there is still so much for me to learn. You have so much to teach me. Calm my heart this morning, and quiet my thoughts. Help me to wait and to listen for Your direction. Thank You for Your instruction to "walk as Jesus walked." To be like Christ is a challenge, but Your promise is that, "I can do all things through Christ who strengthens me" (Phil. 4:13). Fulfill Your purpose through my life as I daily abide in You. In Jesus' name. Amen.

The Same Commandment

Brethren, I write no new commandment to you, but an old commandment which you have had from the beginning. The old commandment is the word which you heard from the beginning. (1 John 2:7)

Thank You, Lord, for precious quiet time with You. The stillness of this hour allows me to reflect. Time does not stand still, and so I thank You for a focused, inward desire to make this day count for You.

Thank you for the teaching of Your Word, and the reminder that You continue to teach the same commandment You have taught from the beginning.

The simplicity of Your word is easily understood— that we are to love one another. Thank You for the life this commandment continues to spark in me. Let my heart be on fire for You today—so on fire that Your love through me will be miraculous and contagious! In Jesus' name. Amen.

What's True in Jesus Is True in Us

Again, a new commandment I write to you, which thing is true in Him and in you, because the darkness is passing away, and the true light is already shining. (1 John 2:8)

I look forward to this day with great expectancy, Lord, because Your Word tells me that "the darkness is passing away, and the true light is already shining." The light and life which You continue to impart causes me to know it will not be an ordinary day! I set my heart to serve You today, and let Your precious light shine through my life.

Your Word is like a new discovery this morning, as it stirs new life within me and reflects Your light on the outside. Help me to walk boldly in this new light today. Thank You that what is true in Jesus is true in me. Thank You that darkness is past, and the true Light lights up my life because Jesus has taken up residence within! In Jesus' name. Amen.

Light or Darkness

He who says he is in the light, and hates his brother, is in darkness until now. (1 John 2:9)

Father, at times the world seems so full of hate and envy. The competitive edge sought by people, organizations, clubs, families, and yes, even between husbands and wives, seems to push aside Your commandment for us to love one another. Thank You for reminding me once again to love with unconditional love.

It is easy to judge others, especially by what they say or do, but I know this isn't the way You would have me treat them. That behavior makes me no better than the one who hates, for I am judging. I desire to walk in Your light, so help me refrain from judging others, especially those who judge me. With Your help, I want to forgive, for hatred and judgmental attitudes toward others push out the light, and without light, the darkness takes over.

Draw me close to Yourself, and fill me with Your unconditional, conciliatory love. Let Your light so shine through me that others are attracted to You, dear Lord. In Jesus' name. Amen.

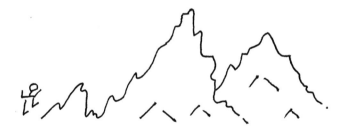

How beautiful on the mountains are the feet of those who bring good news. —Isaiah 52:7 NIV

He Lights Our Path

*He who loves his brother abides in the light,
and there is no cause for stumbling in him.
(1 John 2:10)*

Thank You, Lord God, for the security I feel in the warmth of Your love! Your love not only surrounds me, but it also permeates my being as I sit before You in worship and adoration. Your steadfast promise to me today is that if I love the brethren, then I abide in the light. I do love my brethren because Your miraculous, powerful, unconditional love is working daily in me!

Thank You, Father, for Your abiding love and the warm light that is available day after day. Thank You for the promise that if I will walk in this light, I will not stumble. I want to live and walk in Your light throughout the day. Fill me to overflowing, so that I will be able to help spread Your kingdom throughout the earth. In Jesus' name. Amen.

Darkness Has Blind Eyes

But he who hates his brother is in darkness and walks in darkness, and does not know where he is going, because the darkness has blinded his eyes. (1 John 2:11)

Many members of the body of Christ today are saying that in the earth, darkness is growing darker, and light is growing brighter. We do see witness of Satanic activity increasingly around us. Lord God, the Body of Christ must stand strong in this hour. Many devices are being used in the world to convince people that Christian beliefs are old-fashioned, outdated, outmoded, and antiquated.

O Lord, help us all become sincere men, women, and youth of Your Word. Hate has increased in our world, as can be seen by all the recent incidents of road rage and other types of violent activity. Your words ring even truer when I think of those situations—"He that hates his brother is in darkness, and walks in darkness, and does not know where he is going, because the darkness has blinded his eyes." Lord God, help me spend time with You daily in learning, waiting, worshipping, and praising You. Let me reflect the brilliance of Your love today. I want to make a difference in my small part of this world! In Jesus' name. Amen.

How beautiful on the mountains are the feet of those who bring good news. —Isaiah 52:7 NIV

Edifiers Like John

I write to you, little children...fathers...young men... (1 John 2:12–14)

Thank You, Lord, for the apostle John who called all people, regardless of age, to grow and mature in You. He reassured the children of their salvation and their ability to surrender to You. He encouraged and edified fathers because of their wisdom, and he praised young men because they overcame temptations, were strong, and let God's Word abide in them.

Lord, help the body of Christ have the faith of children, the wisdom of fathers, and the courage of youth! Instill in me, O Lord, the qualities needed to serve You well. Help me become an edifier and an encourager of all people, regardless of age. Help me to realize that as I edify others, I become a powerful instrument in building Your kingdom!

Help me surrender myself to You as the great apostle John surrendered himself daily. Perform Your good works through me this day and I'll give You all the praise. In Jesus' name. Amen.

Attraction to the World

Do not love the world or the things in the world.
If anyone loves the world, the love of the Father
is not in him. (1 John 2:15)

*F*ather, help me relate to the world and be involved in it, but avoid its pitfalls by becoming too strongly attracted to worldly things. How strong the temptations can be which chip away relentlessly at the integrity upon which our free country was built! How subtle the enemy's words are spoken through magazines, television programs, movies, newspapers, commentators, and others who don't know You!

It might be easier to turn the world aside and tell myself that I should have no involvement. But, Lord, You would have me be in the world, yet not of the world. All around there are murders, abortions, drugs, drunkenness, theft, greed, adultery, divorce, crime, abuse, hunger, prostitution—the list could go on and on. How much easier it would be to turn the world aside and stay uninvolved. Teach me, O God, to be a shining light in the world of darkness, but keep me from the temptation to love the world, for if I love the world, You have said that the love of the Father would not be in me!

Help me assume my portion of responsibility. Give me wisdom to understand how to love the world the way that You would have me to, and to be a force for You in this world. Increase your love within me. Teach me the important things in this life, and let your Spirit of wisdom rest upon me. In Jesus' name. Amen.

The Flesh

For all that is in the world—the lust of the flesh.
(1 John 2:16a)

Lord, how clearly You define the things that are of the world. My flesh, the lust of my eyes, and the pride of my life are of the world and not of You. Help me to understand what "walking in the flesh" truly means. Help me to not think of myself all of the time, to not be selfish with my wants and needs. I know my flesh is selfish and wants only immediate fulfillment. Because I am human, I must contend with my flesh—I must not allow it to influence my thoughts and actions.

Lord, at times, my flesh turns me from Your will to my own so subtly that I am not always aware of it. Only with the help of Your Spirit am I able to control my flesh! Help me put away old habits and desires that I may see You more clearly. Come, Holy Spirit. Be my guide, my assurance, and my strength. I am weak, but I find my strength in You. Make me sensitive to Your leadership. Continue to lead and guide me into all truth. In Jesus' name. Amen.

Lust of the Eyes

For all that is in the world...the lust of the eyes...
(1 John 2:16b)

*D*ear Lord, thank You for taking away the mystery of what is of the world and what is of You. Your Word truly is sharper than any two-edged sword (Heb. 4:12). Your Word is what allows me to discern the difference between the world and Your path to take. How easy it might be to ignore 1 John 2:16 which defines the world and all of its characteristics—the sin of our flesh, the lust of our eyes, and pride.

I generally attribute Your admonishment to avoid the "lust of the eyes" as applicable to men, adultery, prostitutes, and things that are sexually immoral. But what are You truly saying to myself and to the body of Christ? Do my eyes lust? They surely do! The lust of my eyes causes me to look upon things that belong to others and covet them for myself. The lust of my eyes causes me to purchase things that give me immediate gratification without thinking through the long-range financial consequences. Convict me of my personal sin in this area, and set my thoughts aright today. Thank You for this opportunity to confess my sins. Thank You for the strength that comes from daily cleansing in Your Word. I love You, my Lord and my Christ! In Jesus' name. Amen.

How beautiful on the mountains are the feet of those who bring good news. —Isaiah 52:7 NIV

The Pride of Life

*For all that is of the world...the pride of life—
is not of the Father but is of the world.
(1 John 2:16c)*

Lord, thank You for Your Word which was inspired by Your Holy Spirit. Help us to understand and discern correctly what You mean in Your Word. When You spoke of the "world" and of the things of the world, You were also speaking of Satan and those things under his domain, sins such as the lust of the flesh, the lust of the eyes, and the pride of life.

How often am I motivated to do or not to do something because of the wrong kind of pride? I am not immune from Satan's devices for I still am a human living in a world full of sin. Lord, forgive my pride, and help me grow in humility. I want to grow in the kind of humility that comes from knowing You and loving You deeply. Hold me close to You today. Teach me again, Your discernment so that I may continue to live in the world but not be a part of it. In Jesus' name. Amen.

Passing Things

And the world is passing away, and the lust of it; but he who does the will of God abides forever. (1 John 2:17)

*I*t is pure joy to settle into a quiet time with You, Lord. Thank You for the excitement of new beginnings at the start of each new day! As I consider this day before me, how delightful it is to experience an inward feeling of wonder. What will the day bring? What surprises are in store? As Your child, I marvel at the work of Your hands and wonder what You have in store for me today.

Thank You for a good night's rest and the joy of feeling alive in You! Thank You for these quiet moments when I am able to center my feelings and thoughts on You, Father God. You remind me, again, everything that is of the world—including the lust of the flesh, the lust of the eyes, and the pride of life—will pass away. How fleeting is our life on earth and the things that clamor for our attention often temporal in nature.

Help me to do a good, eternal work today, something that will count for Your eternal kingdom and for Your glory. I want to be Your person in the world, love the world with Your kind of love, but not be "of" the world. Thank you for your promise that "the world will pass away, but we who do Your will will live forever with you." Lead me through another exciting day, Lord. Keep me in the world, but keep my concentration on You. I give you all praise and glory! In Jesus' name. Amen.

Antichrists Are Here

Little children, it is the last hour; and as you have heard that the Antichrist is coming, even now many antichrists have come, by which we know that it is the last hour. (1 John 2:18)

You have created another day, Lord, and what You create is clean, and good, and pure. Your Word tells us that the world is evil and that it shall soon pass away. Help us in the body of Christ to feel an urgency about Your work! I was born for such a time as this. I was saved in order to follow Christ and His commands. Lord, You have a very special job for me to do on this earth. Please reveal Your plans and purposes for my life. In these troubled times, men's hearts are dark, and daily there seems to be greater propensity for evil. And yet I remain encouraged because You tell us that the world is full of antichrists and that this is proof we are in the last days.

You promised that "whatever is born of God over-comes the world and this is the victory that has overcomes the world—our faith!" (1 John 1:4). Thank you, Lord, for the assurance that goodness shall reign despite increased evil and so many antichrists! Help me walk in the love of Jesus Christ, for His love is powerful and overcomes the world. Fill me with Your powerful love and cover me with the precious blood of Jesus. Thank You that I walk without fear and shine God's light wherever I go. Thank You for the light of love that dispels darkness. Help me make a difference until You come. Come, Lord Jesus! In Jesus' name. Amen.

Belonging

They went out from us, but they were not of us; for if they had been of us, they would have continued with us; but they went out that they might be made manifest, that none of them were of us. (1 John 2:19)

*T*hank You for the feeling of belonging that accompanies me as a child of Yours, O Lord. I know that I belong to You, and Your love is steadfast, no matter what I may be feeling. Thank you for precious church which binds me to a wonderful family—a family that physically and spiritually encircles me constantly with love and support.

Lord, sometimes Christians do seem to fall away, and it's difficult to understand. Your Word tells us that when some turn away or leave the body of Christ, it is because they didn't belong in the first place. Help me to help those who don't really know You. Enable me to so love them that they are drawn into a relationship with You; a relationship which gives assurance of eternal love and eternal existence with You. Give me wisdom, Lord, that I become convincingly authentic for Your glory. In Jesus' name. Amen.

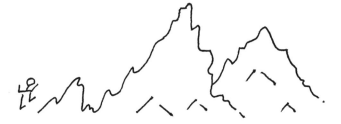

How beautiful on the mountains are the feet of those who bring good news. —Isaiah 52:7 NIV

Anointed for Service

But you have an anointing from the Holy One...
(1 John 2:20a)

Lord God, how little I seem to understand about You, the Holy Spirit, and the anointing, until You bring me back to Your Word and cause me to stop, reread, and listen to what You have to teach. Your presence, Your Holy Spirit comes to me when I begin to see Your holiness and repent of my sins. Now I understand the anointing comes when the Spirit begins to lead and guide the believer!

Thank you for your promise, "Now it is God who makes both us and you stand firm in Christ. He anointed us, set His seal of ownership on us, and put His Spirit in our hearts as a deposit, quaranteeing what is to come" (2 Cor. 1:21 NIV).

Just as Jesus received the anointing of the Spirit when He was baptized, and You gave him commission for His service as Messiah; so we are baptized by Your Spirit and anointed for service in the kingdom of God! O

Lord God, thank you for the way you challenge me daily in this beautiful relationship with You! Thank You for teaching me Your truth, and thank You for the anointing of the Holy Spirit. Strengthen me to walk in it today. In Jesus' name. Amen.

How beautiful on the mountains are the feet of those who bring good news. —Isaiah 52:7 NIV

Knowing Truth

...and you know all things. (1 John 2:20b)

*H*eavenly Father, how gracious You are. How privileged I am to be Your child! Thank You for Your Holy Spirit who indwells, leads, guides, comforts, and meets my needs when I seek solace and reassurance. How weak my faith seems to be at times, but how strong is Your indwelling Spirit! He gives illumination to my questions and understanding when I pray. Thank You for the anointing I received with the indwelling of Your Holy Spirit. Proof of Your indwelling is the knowledge You give me, so often far surpassing what I would know in and of myself. How I praise You for that!

Your promise is that "Eye has not seen nor ear heard, nor have entered the heart of man the things which God has prepared for those who love Him. But God has revealed them to us through His Spirit!" (1 Cor. 2:9–10a). Thank you for wisdom given as I seek daily. I listen to You whisper wisdom and knowledge through Your Word. Lord God, the power of Your word, and

Your very presence that comes through spending time with You never ceases to astound me. My heart looks up to You in praise and thanksgiving! In Jesus' name. Amen.

How beautiful on the mountains are the feet of those who bring good news. —Isaiah 52:7 NIV

Truth or Antichrists

I have not written to you because you do not know the truth, but because you know it, and that no lie is of the truth. (1 John 2:21)

Good morning, Lord! What a privilege it is to greet You in this new day. Thank You for the anticipation of meeting with You in my heart, and the promise that Your mercies are new each morning. I yield myself to You and to Your Spirit. Recreate Yourself within me as I surrender myself to You.

Thank you for yesterday and the victories You have given me in the past. Forgive me where I have failed You, or did not listen to Your still, small voice. Grow Your amazing grace within me. Give me ears to hear You, and a heart to receive You in Your fullness this day, Lord. I will be careful to recognize You in everything that I do today.

Thank you for the reassurance that I understand the truth. I can acknowledge Your truth because of Your new life within. Thank You for Your abiding Spirit within me who helps me recognize Your truth and keeps me from becoming deceived by antichrists who deny the Godhead. Help me to declare Your truth today as You have revealed it to me. I want to be a faithful follower of You. Lead me in Your ways and continue to show me Your truth. In Jesus' name. Amen.

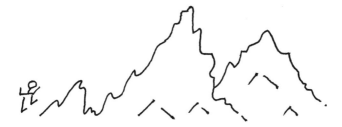

How beautiful on the mountains are the feet of those who bring good news. —Isaiah 52:7 NIV

Liars and Deceivers

Who is a liar but he who denies that Jesus is the Christ? He is antichrist who denies the Father and the Son. Whoever denies the Son does not have the Father either... (1 John 2:22–23)

*F*ather, You say, unmistakably, that those who deny that Jesus is the Christ, the Messiah, the Savior of the world, the Son of God, and our Redeemer, are liars and deceivers. O God, continue to draw all persons to Yourself. Let the convicting power of Your Holy Spirit so flow through our churches that hearts are strangely warmed with Your gentle conviction! Let Your people be so in tune with Your Spirit that entire congregations will be overwhelmed, redeemed, cleansed, and filled with Your sweet presence.

Lord Jesus, I know You are coming soon! Let me be continuously about Your business. Cause me to be fit for Your use today.

I give all honor and glory to You Father, Son, and Holy Spirit. Reign abundantly in my life. I receive Your love into my heart. Help me to share it with others graciously. Just as Your Word is sharper than a two-edged sword, so let Your love, flowing through me, help draw the deceivers, the liars, the "antichrists" into an understanding and acceptance of You, our wonderful Lord and Savior! In Jesus' name. Amen.

How beautiful on the mountains are the feet of those who bring good news. —Isaiah 52:7 NIV

Faithfulness

Therefore let that abide in you which you heard from the beginning. If what you heard from the beginning abides in you, you also will abide in the Son and in the Father. (1 John 2:24)

Thank You, Lord God, for reminding us again and again that the world is not our friend. We exist in this world and must always live in it, yet we need to be wise enough to avoid its pitfalls. I pray for the body of Christ, that we seek Your wisdom regularly to help us avoid the traps and snares of the enemy. In this time of seeking You, You will help us recognize the subtle traps of the enemy!

Television, radio, magazines, all of these are filling our airwaves with sex and violence. In addition to this overwhelming influence from the media, our children and youth are being directly targeted by Satan while we Christians and law-abiding citizens stand idly by and watch!

Your Word tells us to remember what we have learned and hold fast to it. How easy it is to stray from our close relationship with You and become involved with wrong thinking and ideas. Thank You for wooing us back to Yourself when our flesh is pulling us the other direction. Set a fire under the body of Christ! Spur us into action so that we will accept our responsibility and become involved in our society, making a difference for You! Remind us to turn to Your word daily to receive of Your strength and to prayer for the cleansing of our sins. Help us turn to You for wisdom to live in these days with courage and effectiveness. Hold us closely to Yourself, and keep us faithful in our service to You, for it's in the precious name of Jesus we pray. Amen.

Eternal Life

And this is the promise that He has promised us—eternal life. (1 John 2:25)

Lord, my walk with You is so rich and exciting! Thank You for the promise of eternal life You have given to me in Your Word. When I was a child, I wondered, with excitement, if there really was a pot of gold at the end of the rainbow. Now, as Your child, I wonder, with excitement, about spending eternity with You! The difference is that now I know eternal life is true. I'm enjoying eternal life now, and the best is yet to come! What a comfort to contemplate living forever and ever the life that began when I was born again.

Thank You, Lord, for this new, eternal life which continues to stir within me daily. Thank You for Your Word which teaches me how to guard and nurture my new life. And Lord God, thank You that this eternal life that You have promised is like a rainbow. Your presence hovers over me, and gives me constant incentive to continue my walk with You. Thank you for new heights, new freedom and the excitement of new elevations in this pilgrim walk!

All fear of death is gone because Your resurrection has given me eternal life! One day I shall die, but I will go instantly to heaven to spend eternity in Your presence. Thank You for Your promise, that You will raise up my mortal body at the last day! Keep me close to Yourself, and guide my feet in this present eternal life, until I go to spend eternity with You! In Jesus' name. Amen.

Seduction

These things I have written to you concerning those who try to deceive you. (1 John 2:26)

*F*ather God, just as there were opponents to orthodox teachings when this passage of scripture was written to the body of Christ, so there are opponents to orthodox teachings in the church today. Awaken me to any erroneous teachings that might infiltrate the body of Christ today. Give wisdom to our church leaders, and return us all to our roots, the true teachings of the Scriptures.

Help everyone take responsibility for the discipleship of young believers, teaching and admonishing the babes in Christ to spend time daily with You in Your Word and in prayer. Help the church retain its orthodox teachings, the true teachings of Jesus Christ. Forgive us all for giving all responsibility to our pastors and church leaders when each believer has a responsibility to You! Instill an urgency in my heart to witness Your truth convincingly and lovingly today. In Jesus' name. Amen.

The Anointing

But the anointing which you have received from Him abides in you, and you do not need that anyone teach you; but as the same anointing teaches you concerning all things, and is true, and is not a lie, and just as it has taught you, you will abide in Him. (1 John 2:27)

Lord, what a wonderful mystery Your anointing is. I know through experience that You give special abilities at different times when I am earnestly seeking Your face and am walking in obedience to You. You give understanding when I have no understanding. I praise You for enabling me through your Holy Spirit. Your Holy Spirit gives me unusual understanding when I study, listen, and wait upon You. This is Your anointing operating in my life!

Your Word tells me that I have received an anointing, and that this anointing teaches truth as I abide in You. Help me rely upon your commandments to lead me into all truth. Just as Jesus breathed upon His disciples and they received the Holy Spirit, so I have the

Holy Spirit within me to give me help and understanding when I seek Him. Thank You for the anointing and the promise that this anointing abides in me. Quicken my ears to hear Your voice today. In Jesus' name. Amen.

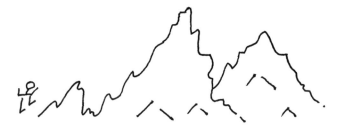

How beautiful on the mountains are the feet of those who bring good news. —Isaiah 52:7 NIV

Jesus Is Coming!

And now, little children, abide in Him, that when He appears, we may have confidence and not be ashamed before Him at His coming. (1 John 2:28)

Yes, Lord Jesus, You are coming! This is good reason to stay in close contact with You. Help me, Lord, to live and to walk in You, so that when You come, I will be able to face You boldly, with a clear conscience.

Create in me a confidence that cannot be shaken— a mountain of confidence that comes from walking in Your abiding love. Thank You for Your promise, "...In returning and rest shall you be saved; In quietness and confidence shall be your strength" (Is. 30:15a).

Help me do and say the things that You would have me do and say. Quicken my heart anew, dear Lord, as I walk through this day for Your glory. Thank You for helping me do the right things, the things You would have me to do. I wait upon You to hear Your voice. In Jesus' name. Amen.

A Pilgrim's Prayer

O, Lord, the war rages between light and darkness. I see the unfairness and cruelty in the world, and I wonder when Your intervention will come.

In the meantime, O, Lord, teach me Your ways. Instill the truths of Your Word into my heart. Fill me with Your strength to withstand the powers of the enemy. And most of all, give me wisdom to discern the face of evil. Help me to see through the devices of the enemy, who so stealthily sneaks up from behind and tempts me to take a different path than the one You would have me to take.

Teach the body of Christ how to stand when the darkness surrounds from every side. Give encouragement to the body of Christ. Let Your disciples of today speak boldly and with convictions that cannot be refuted.

O, God, steady me in Your will this day. Fill my heart with courage and conviction strong enough that I might leave my safety net and venture into those places that so desperately need Your light. Let courage be in my heart to overcome the camps of the enemy. Let me show a needy world that You are indeed strong in Your people.

Today, give me an opportunity to share Your love with someone in need. Search me, O, Lord, and cleanse away any sinfulness so that I may move willingly and without hesitation when You speak. Work through my hands and my feet. Bring glory to Your Name through my life. I pray in the mighty name of Jesus Christ and for His sake. Amen.

Chapter Three
A Pilgrim's Prayer

Father, it is so easy to neglect daily quiet time with You. Days can go by, and I feel rushed into my days because my "to do list" seems so long and formidable. Help me to make the most of my time, so that I am a good steward of the days You have given to me.

Forgive me for letting the enemy pressure me into submission to his plan, which is to neglect my time with You. Lord, when I try to do things without You, my accomplishments are futile and incomplete. Step in, Lord Jesus, and bring peace and order once again!

When will I learn? When will I see, once and for all, that my days are not pleasing in Your sight unless You have full reign? I pause before You now, Lord God. Touch my heart, touch all of me for I am nothing without You. My thoughts and plans fall short if they are not governed by Your Spirit!

I surrender completely to You today. Take my hands, my feet, my mind, my thoughts—take all of me unto

Yourself so that I might be filled once again with Your overpowering love. Make me an instrument for Your use today. Rejuvenate everything about me so that I exude nothing other than Yourself. Thank You for hearing my prayer. In Jesus' name, I pray. Amen.

How beautiful on the mountains are the feet of those who bring good news. —Isaiah 52:7 NIV

Miraculous Love!

Behold what manner of love the Father has bestowed on us, that we should be called children of God. (1 John 3:1a)

*P*recious Father, again this morning I contemplate Your miraculous love. I am unable to truly express the awe, surprise, and wonder I feel when I consider how much You love with undying love. Your Word says, "Behold!" That says it all. "*Behold*, what manner of love the Father has bestowed upon us, that we should be called children of God!"

Thank You for coming in the flesh. Thank You for Jesus Christ, Your Son, who shed His innocent blood that my sins could be forgiven. Thank You for the innocent Lamb who made it possible for me to come boldly into Your throne room and say, "Abba Father!" Thank You for, "Your Spirit which bears witness with our spirit that we are children of God" (Ro. 8:16). What wondrous love You have for us! In Jesus' name. Amen.

Recognition

*Therefore the world does not know us, because
it did not know Him. (1 John 3:1b)*

Lord Jesus, thank You for this sweet reunion with You
and Your Word this morning. What a privilege it is
to open the Bible and read Your Word. Your words are
as alive and anointed this morning as they were when
they were given by You and recorded by man thou-
sands of years ago.

Thank You for faith and for the freedom to exercise
my will to believe. Strengthen my faith today Lord, as I
yield to You.

Thank You for warning me that the world will not
recognize or understand my faith, just as they did not
recognize You so long ago. I look to You today, Lord
God, for recognition, and thank You for Your recognition and undying love! In Jesus' name. Amen.

Equality in Christ

Beloved, now we are children of God...
(1 John 3:2a)

Thank You, Lord, for calling Your believers, "children of God." Thank You that gender has nothing to do with Your expression of love toward humanity. Equality reigns as far as Jesus is concerned for men, women, girls, and boys in the kingdom of God. Hallelujah!

How glorious that discovery was in my growth process when I discovered my true worth in Jesus Christ. Jesus is no respecter of persons and loves all humans—male and female—equally. What freedom exists in this knowledge! Help us all as Christian men and women to share that attitude of equality toward one another so Your kingdom may come on earth as it is in heaven. In Jesus' name. Amen.

We Shall Be Like Him

But we know that when He is revealed, we shall be like Him, for we shall see Him as He is. (1 John 3:2b)

Lord God, what a wonderful mystery, this relationship I have with Jesus Christ! How intangible my faith is, and yet it is so real, so comforting, so powerful! Thank You that I am changing day by day into the very image of Jesus Christ. I myself cannot cause this change to occur, but instead, You fashion me according to Your will. Help me today as I seek Your holy face. Help me open wide my heart and soul for You. Forgive me, cleanse me, wash me until I am whiter than snow!

Lord, I don't always understand Your miraculous workings in my life and in the lives of other believers, but I know that because of Your mercy and grace, changes for the good are taking place. Thank You for promising that when Jesus appears we shall be like Him, for we shall see Him as He is! Thank You for this holy day in which I can live for You. Guide my footsteps in it, and make me a blessing to others. I love You, Lord. In Jesus' name I pray. Amen.

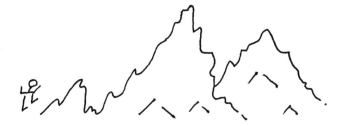

How beautiful on the mountains are the feet of those who bring good news. —Isaiah 52:7 NIV

Purification

And everyone who has this hope in Him purifies himself, just as He is pure. (1 John 3:3)

Today is a day You have made, Lord, and I rejoice in it. Thank You for another day in which to serve You. Your Word continues to enrich my soul and encourage my spirit. I am excited to serve You day by day! The motivational power of Your love brings me to my knees in a desire to know You even better.

Thank you, O Lord, for the desire to worship You. Thank You for the desire to live a righteous life. Only You, by Your Spirit, can facilitate this process in my heart. I yield myself once again today—body, soul, and spirit. Holy are You, God of power and might! Have Your way in my life. I want only You today. Touch me, O Lord, and make me fit for my Master's use. In Jesus' name. Amen.

Sin

Whoever commits sin also commits lawlessness, and sin is lawlessness. And you know that He was manifested to take away our sins, and in Him there is no sin. (1 John 3:4–5)

Lord, thank You for Your Word that tells me I am a sinner when I fail to obey your commandments. I need to have this reminder in my life. Thank You for Your Word that tells me exactly what sin is. Heavenly Father, forgive all of my transgressions. Cleanse me anew, and fill me with Your Spirit so that I may be about Your business today. Thank You that when I am the weakest, You are ready to make me strong—where I have the greatest need, You will fill the void.

Thank You that, with Your enabling, I may not transgress Your law. The words of Your law are not grievous, but full of love, mercy, kindness, and grace! Thank You for Jesus Christ who did not sin and was offered by You to take away my sin. Dear Lord, I thank You that I do have power over sin because of Christ's sacrifice and the power of the Holy Spirit who helps me to overcome temptation. Thank You that "there is therefore no condemnation to those who are in Christ Jesus, who do not walk according to the flesh, but according to the Spirit" (Romans 8:1). I reach gratefully for Your hand of mercy and for Your everlasting love! In Jesus' name. Amen.

How beautiful on the mountains are the feet of those who bring good news. —Isaiah 52:7 NIV

Abiding in God

Whoever abides in Him does not sin. Whoever sins has neither seen Him nor known Him. (1 John 3:6)

Lord God, Your unfailing Word has all the answers that I need, if I will just spend time in it every day. Forgive me for the times I rush into the day without spending precious, unhurried time in Your Word, in prayer, and waiting upon You. You are so faithful to cleanse, fill, and strengthen me when I give You the opportunity to do so.

Your Word tells me that if I am *abiding* in you, I won't sin. To "abide" can encompass such a broad spectrum of meaning. I want to abide in You to the fullest extent! Help me continue to be close to You in an enduring, lasting, persistent, and strengthened way, as I am faithful in absorbing Your Word daily. Thank You for Your commandment that tells me plainly that the one who doesn't abide in You hasn't truly seen You, nor known You. O, Jesus, I've seen You, and I know You; therefore, I know how to abide in You.

Thank You for hearing my prayer, and giving strength and wisdom to me for Your service today. Thank You for time to spend in Your precious, anointed Word! Thank You for the privilege I have of coming to You in prayer, and the knowledge that You are always waiting and listening for praise and petitions from Your children. Thank You for time to wait upon You, and the mystery and fullness of Your Presence in that time of waiting. I praise Your holy name, Jesus! Amen.

To Be Righteous

Little children, let no one deceive you. He who practices righteousness is righteous, just as He is righteous. (1 John 3:7)

*P*recious Lord, help me wait upon You today. Help me to realize anew that You are willing to lead, guide, and direct me into all truth. Sometimes it is hard to discern Your voice. I can be too anxious, and too easily caught up in human rationale. Lord, I hunger and thirst after Your righteousness. I want to follow Your commandments which instruct me to become like Jesus.

Forgive me for usurping Your authority. O, Lord, I want to hear what You are trying to teach me. Give me wisdom to live in today's world, and help me to avoid any compromise of Your commandments. Give me a discerning spirit today so that I might not be deceived by the enemy. Give me the courage I need to do and say the right things. In Jesus' name. Amen.

Jesus Destroys Satan's Works

But if you keep on sinning, it shows you belong to Satan, who since he first began to sin has kept steadily at it. But the Son of God came to destroy the works of the devil. (1 John 3:8 TLB)

Lord God, it seems to be a hard word You give today when You say, "if we keep on sinning, it shows we belong to Satan." You make it so plain when You say the devil sinned from the beginning. That is why the Son of God was given for the world; so that He would destroy the devil's works. Lord God, Your teaching makes it clear: I either serve the devil by sinning, or I serve You by obeying Your commands!

Help me to walk in Your love today. Help me to see and understand, clearly, the difference between right and wrong. Thank You for Your Holy Spirit who brings quick conviction when I'm guilty of wrong thoughts, wrong speech, or wrong behavior.

Come Holy Spirit, be my guide today. Teach me the difference between right and wrong. Make me strong enough to cease making excuses for sinfulness, and give me the courage to accept responsibility for my deeds. Lead me in Your steps today, for I want to please You all day long. You alone are infinitely wise and worthy to be praised! In Jesus' name. Amen.

How beautiful on the mountains are the feet of those who bring good news. —Isaiah 52:7 NIV

God's Guarantee Against Sin

*Whoever has been born of God does not sin,
for His seed remains in him; and he cannot sin,
because he has been born of God. (1 John 3:9)*

*T*hank You, God, for Your most precious promise in Your Word today: "Whoever has been born of God does not sin." Lord, there was a time when I could commit sin, and it really didn't bother me. Thank You for your indwelling presence that no longer allows sinful activity in my life anymore. Thank You for that quickening which causes me to turn from sinful thoughts, which lead to actions that are sins against You.

And thank You, Lord, that if I do sin, You are willing to forgive and cleanse me from all unrighteousness. Thank You for my precious advocate, Jesus Christ, who is with the Father and makes intercession for me continually.

As I go into this day, strengthen me where I am the weakest. Keep me from judging others, and let Your hand of mercy continue to rest upon my soul. How precious is Your love. How wide is your mercy. Let this love and mercy be mirrored in the ministry You will accomplish through me today. In Jesus' name. Amen.

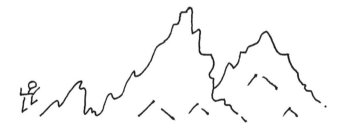

How beautiful on the mountains are the feet of those who bring good news. —Isaiah 52:7 NIV

The Devil's Children Versus God's Children

> *In this the children of God and the children of the devil are manifest: Whoever does not practice righteousness is not of God, nor is he who does not love his brother. For this is the message that you heard from the beginning, that we should love one another not as Cain who was of the wicked one and murdered his brother. And why did he murder him? Because his works were evil and his brother's righteous. Do not marvel, my brethren, if the world hates you. (1 John 3:10–13)*

Father, Your Word is clear: Children of the devil do not do right things. They do not love others. Children of the devil proclaim themselves to be such by being sinners and doing unlovely things. Cain had no love for his brother and killed him. Not only did Cain not love his brother, he took actions of hatred and killed his brother!

Thank You, Lord, for showing me this dichotomy so clearly—that is that evil is loveless and hates goodness. Evil hates and destroys. Loving You wholeheartedly brings contempt and hatred from the world. You said not to be surprised when this occurs. But You are greater than the world, and Your love always triumphs! Thank You that I experience victory through You. Your love conquers darkness, hate, and all things the devil continually brings my way. Touch and fill me today, for Your glory. In Jesus' name. Amen.

Love Amazing, Love Divine!

We know that we have passed from death to life, because we love the brethren. (1 John 3:14a)

Lord God, no matter how much I learn about You, Your Word keeps returning me to this one truth, that we are to love one another. How amazing is this love You have bestowed upon me. It fills me with empathy and helps me love others, even those who despise me!

Thank You for the power of that love which accomplishes so many things. It helps me hope when all looks dismal. It gives me courage when things look dark. It helps me forgive when I've been hurt. It adds zest to drudgery, and light to dark days.

Thank You for Your abounding hope that is fueled by Your gift of love—boundless love which You give so freely! Help me, today, to share Your plentiful, amazing, divine love to a misguided and confused world. Help me always to remember where this love comes from. Lord, keep me in the shadow of Your wings. In Jesus' precious name. Amen.

Death to Life!

Whoever hates his brother is a murderer, and you know that no murderer has eternal life abiding in him. (1 John 3:15)

*F*ather, Your Word makes it so plain as to our soul's condition: We know that we have passed out of death into life, because we love the brethren. He who does not love abides in death, and anyone who hates his brother is a murderer and does not have eternal life abiding in him!

Thank You for taking me from a life of death into a life of love for others. Before I came into a relationship with Jesus Christ, I was living a life of death, but didn't even realize it. I was sometimes the recipient of hate and sometimes returned that hate to others!

Now, because You've come into my heart, and are in the process of changing me, it seems incredible that in the midst of all the evil in the world, I love and have a deep concern for sinners. This is You at work in my life! Because of Your special love given in this new life I understand better the command, "if you love those who love you, what credit is that to you? For even sinners love those who love them" (Luke 6:32).

Thank You for helping me love instead of judging the sinner. You give me great confidence that by loving instead of judging, by accepting others just as they are, I can help make a big difference in our world! In Jesus' name. Amen.

The Comforter Is Here

*By this we know love, because He laid down
His life for us. And we also ought to lay down
our lives for the brethren. (1 John 3:16)*

What a glorious day when I first realized You, Jesus, laid down Your life, not only for the world as a whole, *but for me*! The personal realization melted my heart, and You rushed in. Lord, continue to come into my heart in greater dimensions. How happy that day was when I wept tears of repentance and tears of joy! How cleansing, how liberating, and how comforting it was to experience Your presence. The promised Comforter made Himself real, and I felt His warmth.

Just as Jesus promised, not only has the Holy Spirit come, He never leaves or forsakes me. What love You have! Love that sacrificed innocent blood for the human race! Love that stays close by to lead, guide, and comfort. How can I be so deserving? I can't. These things are only available to me through Your grace and mercy.

And now, Lord, You do command that I lay down my life for others in the same way. In myself, I cannot love that way, but I want to. I cannot give in that way, but I want to. Thank You for challenging me daily toward this lofty goal; and thank You for guiding me steadily through Your Holy Word. Most of all, dear Lord, thank You for encouraging me, even in my weaknesses, with an assurance that You are doing a good work which will not be completed until Jesus Christ returns! Thank You that I'm not the same today as I was yesterday, because You continue to light Your way of love in my life. Come, Holy Spirit. Burn away my selfishness so that I may love my brothers and sisters more deeply. In Jesus' name. Amen.

Love Gives

But whoever has this world's goods, and sees his brother in need, and shuts up his heart from him, how does the love of God abide in him? (1 John 3:17)

Lord, yesterday I saw need, and my heart went out to a poor, crippled man. He opened the door for me, when I should have opened the door for him. He spoke a cheery word to me, when I should have been speaking cheery words to him. Was that You, Lord, showing us sacrificial love?

Father, Your Word tells me that we are to give to the poor and not turn aside wherever there is need. Help me to give of my substance without thought of measuring and keeping back a reserve for myself.

Lead me today, Holy Spirit. Cause me to be more generous. Open my eyes that I may see areas of need. Prompt me to share my goods out of a generous heart. Help me put action to good intentions today. In Jesus' name. Amen.

Gracious Giving

*My little children, let us not love in word or in
tongue, but in deed and in truth. (1 John 3:18)*

Gracious God, what a joy and privilege it is to stand
before You this morning. Gratitude wells up inside
of me when I come to Your throne of grace, for Your
grace is so free and plentiful. Today I come expect-
antly, and already Your words have lifted my spirit to
new heights! Thank You for teaching me again about
the many dimensions of Your love, and how You desire
for Christians to live out this love.

Today, O, Lord, help me to go beyond merely understanding Your love—help me be generous enough
to help those in need. Help me to not only talk of giving, but also help me to actually give to those who
have less than I have. Knowledge is so plentiful, and
talk is so cheap.

Lord, be my catalyst today. Give me courage to act
spontaneously to help others in need. Help me act with
Your love and grace, for it is Your special touch that
will build Your kingdom. In Jesus' name. Amen.

A Clear Conscience

And by this we know we are of the truth...Beloved, if our heart does not condemn us, we have confidence toward God. And whatever we ask we receive from Him, because we keep His commandments and do those things that are pleasing in His sight. (1 John 3:19–21)

*T*hank You, Lord, that You are all truth in this world of increasing debauchery. Thank You for the assurance that I will become a person of truth as I continue to learn of Your love and put into daily practice Your holy instructions.

Thank You for the gift of my conscience, and the way You guide me with this wonderful gift. How I thank You, dear Lord, that the more I learn to love You, and try to live right and do right, the clearer my conscience becomes. Thank You for Your promise that I will be able to come to You without worry, anxiety, or doubt when I am consciously trying to be the person You want me to be.

Help me to keep my priorities straight today—You first, others second, and then my own interests. I delight in Your promise that whatsoever I ask, I receive from You because I keep Your commandments and do those things that are pleasing in Your sight! In Jesus' name. Amen.

How beautiful on the mountains are the feet of those who bring good news. —Isaiah 52:7 NIV

The Spirit Within

Now he who keeps His commandments abides in Him, and He in him. And by this we know that He abides in us, by the Spirit whom He has given us. (1 John 3:24)

Lord Jesus, thank You for all the instructions You have given me in Your Word. Thank You for those who were quickened by Your Spirit and recorded Your Word.

Thank You today for believers who instruct us to witness in the power of Your Spirit—that same promised Spirit who came upon believers gathered in the Upper Room! Thank You that I, too, can witness this power because your Spirit resides within me and gently breathes instructions to me.

I praise You, Lord God, that Jesus promised the disciples they would have the Comforter to lead, guide, and direct them into all truth after His crucifixion. The reality of this presence and leadership builds my faith in You day after day, giving certainty of this truth in my heart. I'm so glad I'm able to say, "I know that You abide in me!" This knowledge is based on reality because the Holy Spirit confirms this truth.

How grateful I am for Your promise, "We know that He lives in us by the Spirit that He has given us." I sing Your praises, Almighty God! In Jesus' name. Amen.

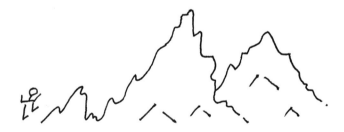

How beautiful on the mountains are the feet of those who bring good news. —Isaiah 52:7 NIV

A Pilgrim's Prayer

O, Father, how weak I feel at times! How vulnerable, how insignificant. I look up to You, dear heavenly Father, as the source of all comfort.

When I am down, You pick me up. When I am weak, You make me strong. When I feel exhausted from the trials in my life, You blow Your soft winds upon me and let me know how much You care. Blow upon me again today, sweet Holy Spirit. Breathe Your refreshing wind for I am weak and tired.

Come today, and refresh me with Your everlasting love. Caress me with a tender touch of confidence—a confidence that can only come from You. Let me know that You are assuredly in control of my life. Give me the stamina to go forward with eagerness into a brand-new day, for You will never fail me, and You will never leave me.

Lord God, I rest in Your presence. With confidence, I await the invigorating power only You can give. Forgive me for ever doubting Your faithfulness, and fill me with purpose for this day. Let Your refreshing touch blow over me until my troubles and concerns fade into the background in the presence of Your awesome power.

Thank You for letting me know these troubles are but for a little while, and through these, You work all things for good. Renew in me a right spirit, O, Lord, and recreate Your redeeming love in me so I'll arise, joyfully, to meet Your challenges for the day!

Keep me close to Yourself, and ever mindful of my need for Your help. In Jesus' name. Amen.

Chapter Four
A Pilgrim's Prayer

Lord Jesus, our world seems so busy and the stress levels of people are so high everywhere. Tempers seem to flare quickly, and patience is so short. People used to be greatly interested in others, but this personal interest in others is waning. So few seem to have time to listen anymore, and courtesy is sometimes lacking.

Sunday worship is an oasis from the world. It is so restful just to sit and concentrate on heavenly things, the body of Christ, and Your tremendous message of love to us. How beautiful the story of Jesus is. How wonderful is the cleansing power of His blood that redeems us. How refreshing the presence of Your Spirit and the contagious joy Your Spirit creates in our fellowship!

Thank You for Your church, Lord, and what it means to us. It is imperfect, just as we are imperfect, because it is comprised of human beings. But its focus is intentional and loving. Thank You that the church exists everywhere, and, for the most part, it strives to be pure. Thank You for souls who are seeking You and for those who love unconditionally. Thank You for pastors of flocks and for those who love You with all their hearts, souls, and minds.

Strengthen pastors and leaders of flocks everywhere. Give them pure motives and the incentive to persist in the ministries to which You've called them. We bind the enemy in the power of Jesus' mighty name from ministers who are called to preach. We use the privileges we have in Jesus to cover the body of Christ with the blood of Jesus!

Lord God, in this world of chaos, You've called us to unity. In this world of misconstrued values and immorality, the voice of Your Holy Spirit speaks to those who will listen. Give us attentive hearts today that we be willing to sit long enough before You, worship You, and wait upon Your Spirit to speak to us. Then give us the courage to obey.

Too often, we have not because we ask not. Too often we seek You, and then fail to obey. Help us with our prayers, our supplications, and our thanksgiving to make our requests be made known to You. Help us to live in harmony with others for the purposes of building Your kingdom.

Teach us Your will through Your Word. Humble us to the point that we are willing to obey the voice of Your Spirit today. Slow us down, Lord. Create in us an even greater desire to press on to the tasks to which we've been called. Forgive our weak intentions and strengthen us all in our resolve to follow You. Lord, especially strengthen our love until it overflows in this stress-filled world. We love You, Lord, with all our hearts, and we bless You in Jesus' name. Amen.

True and False Teachings

Beloved, do not believe every spirit, but test the spirits, whether they are of God; because many false prophets have gone out into the world. (1 John 4:1)

Lord Jesus, there are so many things that are difficult to understand about the spirit world. I believe there were false prophets in the apostle John's day, so there are prophets under the influence of evil spirits in the world today! Give me the wisdom I need to discern Your still, small voice which gives the ability to know the difference between that which is of You and that which isn't of You.

You bring to my mind the words of the Apostle Paul "...where the Spirit of the Lord is, there is freedom" (2 Cor. 3:17 NIV). Remind me again and again that you whisper truth to the inner man. Because of that You will not allow our wills to be superceded by the will of false prophets or teachers without our consent. Keep our eyes upon You, Lord Jesus, and continue to change us from glory to glory.

Your Word tells me there are many false prophets in the world who are teaching untruths. It instructs me that a message should not be accepted just because the messenger seems trustworthy. Your Word says to test the spirits, and causes me to question, "Does this teaching agree that Jesus Christ, God's Son, became a human being?" Or, does this teaching cause me unrest and give vague feelings of uneasiness, or a loss of the peaceful freedom I have in You? Perhaps this check in my spirit is God's way of giving me a warning! Lack of peace and wrong responses as to Jesus' humanity and deity proves certain prophets or teachers are of the antichrist.

Remind me, precious Jesus, that the entrance of Your words into my heart that creates wisdom. It is the entrance of Your words that separate evil from good. Let Your words penetrate my heart and change me from glory to glory. Hold me close as I rest in Your message today. In Jesus' name. Amen.

Antichrists Are Here

> *By this you know the Spirit of God: Every spirit that confesses that Jesus Christ is come in the flesh is of God, and every spirit that does not confess that Jesus Christ has come in the flesh is not of God. And this is the spirit of the Antichrist, which you have heard was coming, and is now already in the world. (1 John 4:2–3)*

*F*ather, more and more each day it seems as if Christianity is becoming considered to be a lifestyle that's out of date and subject to ridicule. Society, in general, used to hold the church sacred and God in high esteem but that is no longer true. "Antichrists" fill our society, and shame no longer seems to exist. But Lord, in the middle of all this hypocrisy, spiritual hunger continues to abound in the hearts of men and women.

Give me Your discernment, Lord. Enable me to listen and judge whether the words spoken by our nation's leaders are of You or of an antichrist. Give wisdom to the body of Christ to discern truth for there are cults and heresies abounding. Your Word instructs us to test the spirits by what is said about Jesus: Is He God in the flesh? Quicken our spiritual ears to listen, read Your Word, and judge whether messages from friends, pulpits, magazines, curriculum, television, and books are authentically from You. Help me to take responsibility for knowing You and Your Word more each day, for You say it is possible to understand more than the ancients if Christians keep close to Your precepts! (Psalm 119:100) I believe that, Lord, with all my heart!

Thank you for the exciting world of the Spirit. Thank You for Your angels sent to minister truth, protect, and guide. Keep me close to Yourself. You are my hiding place and my trustworthy shield. I praise Your holy name. In Jesus' name. Amen.

Truth or Error

He who is in you is greater than he who is in the world. They are of the world. Therefore they speak as of the world, and the world hears them. We are of God. He who knows God hears us; he who is not of God does not hear us. By this we know the spirit of truth and the spirit of error. (1 John 4:4b–6)

*T*hank You, dear Jesus, for the feeling of wholeness created in me as I read the promises in Your Word. Your Word is the bedrock of truth for those who believe. It builds my faith and helps me to learn who You are, why You came to us, and where You are now. It gives direction as to how to live as I walk out my salvation.

Father, You make it so clear that two strong forces are at work in our world. These two forces are the spirit of truth and the spirit of error, and one has no part with the other. The body of Christ cannot expect the world, the spirit of error, to understand or devote any time to the things of God.

Help me, as a believer, not to seek to be understood, but to understand the mindset of the world. Give me a desire to walk in Your peace toward those who do not know You. Shower an abundance of love upon barren hearts today, dear Jesus.

Thank You for Your assurance that what You are building in Your children will withstand the misunderstanding, the persuasions, and the devious methods of the world. We are overcomers in You, Jesus Christ! Teach us to understand our roles as Your messengers. Fill us to overflowing again today so that we are able to share Your quickening presence wherever You lead us. Thank You for the promise that, "Greater is He that is within us, than he that is in the world!" In Jesus' name, amen!

Oh, to Know Him

Beloved, let us love one another, for love is of God; and everyone who loves is born of God and knows God. He who does not love does not know God, for God is love. (1 John 4:7–8)

My heart yearns daily to know You better, O, God. The more I learn of You the more the magnitude of Your might and power seems unfathomable! Thank You for Your Word which describes your characteristics so that we may know You better.

You tell us to love one another, and that if we love one another, we know You, the one who created us and loves us so deeply. I confess that I love You, Lord, but I want to love You more. I am Your child, and I want to love You with the pure delight and trust of a child.

Teach me to love others the way You would have me love them. Help me to see in others what You see in them. I want to see the potential You see in individuals as You are building and grooming them for greater and greater works.

Take my heart, take my hands, take my time, and use them for Yourself throughout the day, Lord. Increase my love for You and for others. Take me a little higher in Your unfathomable love! In Jesus' name. Amen.

How beautiful on the mountains are the feet of those who bring good news. —Isaiah 52:7 NIV

We Live Through Jesus

In this the love of God was manifested toward us, that God has sent His only begotten Son into the world, that we might live through Him. (1 John 4:9)

Lord Jesus, I meditate on Your words, "I in You, and You in Me, and both of us in the Father" (John 17:21–23). What an awesome thought that I, as a believer, can be "in You," the great Creator of the world. How can this be? You promise eternal life through my acceptance of You as Lord and Savior. What a miracle that You come in and dwell in my heart!

Not only are You in me and I in You, but both of us are "in the Father" (John 17:21–23). In 1 John 4:9, Your promise is that "we live through Jesus." Just as Jesus is our heavenly intercessor, and everything we do is sanctioned and sanctified through His intercession for us, so everything we do is done through Him on this earth!

Lord Jesus, I draw near to You today, through reading Your Word and through prayer. Please draw near to me so that I might be Your spokesperson in a needy world. Purify these hands, these thoughts, these feet, my inner desires, cleanse me that I might truly live for You and through You today. I surrender all that I am to You. Let me experience anew the glory of being at one with You. Recreate Yourself in me for Your purposes today. I love You, Lord, with all my heart! In Jesus' name. Amen.

Love Is Gratitude

In this is love, not that we loved God, but that He loved us and sent His Son to be the propitiation for our sins. Beloved, if God so loved us, we also ought to love one another. (1 John 4:10–11)

Lord, you've provided us with a special season. We've enjoyed repeated rains and morning and evening dew. Rays of sunshine stream through the heavy tree foliage in the backyard. The grass gives the impression of dancing as the shimmering sun shines brightly upon the heavy dew drops.

How warm, how inviting this early morning sun! What a welcome sight, the heavy dew! All around, every day, You surround us with Yourself, O Lord! Thank you for sun rays which remind us of your love—all encompassing, bright and yet soft, warm, and penetrating. Thank you for the dew on the grass which is evidence of Your many unexpected blessings.

I open myself to experience the fullness of Your love this morning Lord. Thank you for Your living presence that surrounds us and the miracle of Your living presence inside of us. How glorious the privilege we have of touching, tasting, and experiencing Your goodness!

Jesus, thank You for dying on the cross for me! This is love. This is a true love. Because of this, You command us to love one another. Help me to see opportunities to care, and love, and do good deeds. I want to be a ray of sunshine in someone's life or unexpected dew that will bring a blessing to another person. Help me be a bright and shining, refreshing witness of You! In Jesus' name. Amen.

What Does God Look Like?

No one has seen God at any time. If we love one another, God abides in us, and His love has been perfected in us. (1 John 4:12)

Each spring, vibrant colors in nature, the glorious work of Your hands, declare Your goodness and faithfulness. The grass is green, and the budding, spring flowers are breathtaking. They remind me yet again of Your faithfulness and love. Your goodness is new every morning. You reveal again and again how creative, how new, how fresh, and how miraculous the work of Your hands can be—How great Your love is for us!

Your Word tells us You have never been seen. But I see You, precious Creator. I see You, and I experience ever greater and greater measures of Your love by looking, touching, feeling Your wonders in nature.

Lord God, most precious is seeing and experiencing Your joy and Your love through other people. Open my heart today. I want to experience all that You are through my interactions with others, through talking to You in prayer, through absorbing the colors and wonders of Your creations!

Your promise is that, "If we love one another, God dwells in us, and His love is perfected in us." Perfect Your love in me, O, Lord, so that I can see You more clearly! In Jesus' name. Amen.

How beautiful on the mountains are the feet of those who bring good news. —Isaiah 52:7 NIV

The Inward Witness

By this we know that we abide in Him, and He in us, because He has given us of His Spirit. (1 John 4:13)

Thank You for the dawn of a new day, Lord Jesus, and for Your Holy Spirit which dwells in me. Thank You for the assurance that I am one of Your own.

O, Lord God, make me an instrument of Your peace today. Fill me with Yourself, that I may truly be Your instrument throughout the day. Help me to share Your love with a world that is confused and lost. I praise You for the inward witness that continues to guide me to love a hurting, hungry, and misguided world. Cause me to be a refreshing breath of air wherever You lead me to go.

Teach me again and again that it is not by my own power or might, but everything done for You must be done solely through the prompting of Your Holy Spirit. Lead, guide, prompt, correct, and make me an instrument of Your peace. Fill me to overflowing with Your love. Bring honor and glory to Your name as I surrender myself to Your leadership. Let this day be one in which Your love fills my heart with brightness to be a blessing to others! In Jesus' name. Amen.

How beautiful on the mountains are the feet of those who bring good news. —Isaiah 52:7 NIV

Living Testimonies

And we have seen and testify that the Father has sent the Son as Savior of the world. (1 John 4:14)

Thank You, precious Holy Spirit, for Your indwelling that never leaves or forsakes me. I rejoice in the bubbling, overflowing joy that comes from You. Let this joy be a testimony and its brightness bring life to others throughout the day.

Father, Your Spirit is a living presence within me and a steady influence to guide my path. Without You, I am nothing. You deserve all of the praise for Your goodness and mercy. Thank You for the privilege of walking in that influence. Help me to tell others of this wondrous relationship—a relationship with a living Presence, a living Counselor and Friend, a living Guide who draws near to our hearts when comfort is needed. Help me to have the courage to tell others about the Savior!

Forgive me for the times I have failed to share when You have opened doors for me to share my witness.

Strengthen my resolve to testify of the works that Christ has done in my life. Let my speech today be seasoned and rich with Your grace, my precious Redeemer.

I will be a living testimony today by sharing with others our living Savior, who loves the world with His unfailing love! In Jesus' name. Amen.

How beautiful on the mountains are the feet of those who bring good news. —Isaiah 52:7 NIV

Witness

Whoever confesses that Jesus is the Son of God abides in him, and he in God. (1 John 4:15)

Father, thank You for the power of prayer. I'm so grateful for the ability to come before You daily and confess my shortcomings, for in this confession time You give me strength—strength that comes from opening my heart to You completely and surrendering my human will to Your perfect will.

Not only do I want You to take over the control of my day, but I also desire Your cleansing that will make me a vessel worthy to bring honor and glory to You.

What a blessing to come to You in prayer! Thank You for Your Word that cleanses, inspires, and teaches me the way I should go. Thank You for Your Word that prepares my heart for prayer.

Lord God, today You have told me in Your Word, "Whosoever shall confess that Jesus is the Son of God, God dwells in him and he in God." Give me an urgency to tell others about Jesus, His saving grace, His wonderful love and His abiding presence!

Remind me again, Lord, that there are hurting people who need a witness of Your love! O, God, place them upon the hearts of Your people. Help us be a potent force for You in the church and in the world.

Today, Lord, wherever I am, flow through me in telling the story of Jesus and His love. Let me not be ashamed, but help me to be a witness for You! In Jesus' name. Amen.

The Perfecting Process

God is love, and he who abides in love abides in God, and God in him. Love has been perfected among us in this: that we may have boldness in the day of judgment; because as He is, so are we in this world. (1 John 4:16b–17)

*T*hank You, O, God, for Your perfect love manifested to me through Jesus' sacrifice on the cross. Thank You for Your admonition to be like Jesus and allow that same love to become more and more perfected within my heart. This challenge from You causes me to look ahead to what You have planned for the body of Christ. We will be bold in the day of judgment!

Some days, I can feel unmotivated to do Your will until I remember the process taking place within me— the process of Your perfecting me according to Your love. I remember You are taking me on to higher planes of perfection and desire that I am in You, ministering to a lost and hurting world. Thank You for Your gentle reminders. Thank You for Your renewal process within me. Thank You for the promise that I am not only to know Your love, but I am to constantly believe in Your love, for this is the way to dwell in it—to dwell in You, and You in me!

Thank You for the promise that love is made perfect by dwelling in You, and this will bring boldness in face of judgment, because as You are, so I am to be in this world. Lord, help me dwell in Your love today. Help me be as You are in this world. Thank You for Your great love, and thank You for this ongoing, exciting, perfecting process! In Jesus' name. Amen.

Such Love!

*There is no fear in love; but perfect love casts
out fear, because fear involves torment. But he
who fears has not been made perfect in love.
We love Him because He first loved us.
(1 John 4:18–19)*

*D*ear Lord, forgive me for sometimes neglecting the
time that I should spend with You. Your love is so
amazing, so fulfilling, that it casts out all fear in my
life. As I sit with You now and contemplate the mag-
nificence of Your love, I wonder who can truly understand it?

Lord, You tell me in the scripture for today that perfect love casts out fear. When I have fear, it's because
I'm not allowing You to perfect Your love in my heart!
Lord, I want Your love to operate in and through me to
the perfection that You desire.

Thank you, Lord, for Your growing love inside of
me. There seems to be no limit to that love that You
want to instill inside my heart. Help me to slow down

today, Lord, so that I am able to hear Your still, small voice, teaching, assuring, forgiving, and instructing me in Your ways.

Thank you for first loving me. Thank You that I don't have to prove anything to You in order to be loved by You. Your love is unconditional! You see me just as I am, and yet Your love for me never changes! Thank You for Your grace, mercy, and love. In Jesus' name. Amen.

The Choice

If someone says, "I love God," and hates his brother, he is a liar...he who loves God must love his brother also. (1 John 4:20–21)

Lord, I choose to serve You daily. I keep You uppermost in my thoughts, and I have the best of intentions! How fickle I must seem to You sometimes when I come, much like a child promising to do better, to serve You in the best way I know how. Yet, I fail to love many other people. Lord, some people are harder to love than others! They seem detestable, hateful, mean, arrogant, and deceitful, but yet You tell me I am to love them anyway.

Your Word tells me that I'm a liar if I say I love You but at the same time, am not loving others. My heart convicts me; You command love for the unlovely as well as the lovely. You say, how can I love You whom I've not seen and yet fail to love others I'm able to see?

I have Your commandment: "He who loves God loves his brother also." Lord, help me love the unlovely as well as the lovely. Help me to measure my love for You by the reflection of my love toward others. I need more of Your love in my life today, Lord. Help me to choose to be more loving to everyone! In Jesus' name. Amen.

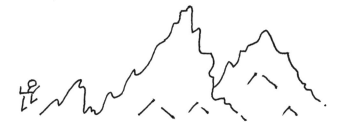

How beautiful on the mountains are the feet of those who bring good news. —Isaiah 52:7 NIV

A Pilgrim's Prayer

*F*ather, we thank You for the work You are doing in the world today. These are exciting times in which to be living in the body of Christ, for Your Spirit is moving throughout our world! You are touching lives in new ways!

By Your Spirit, You are showing the miraculous work of Your hands. You are creating a new excitement which reaches beyond us, our churches, our city, our community, and into the world.

Expand our mindsets so that we may see what You have planned for us, individually, corporately, and throughout our community. Give us the eyes to see Your ways, and help us to understand Your desires. Remold our hearts again and again, so that Your motivations for the body of Christ become our motivations. Help us see and understand ourselves in a new light, and give us a new burden for the body of Christ.

Forgive us for desiring to please our own selves, or only focus on our own church, and our own plans for our own people. Help us see and understand, that it is in worldwide giving to immediate needs that You preserve us. Help us understand how to edify and build up our areas of responsibility, so that we can better give to those around us.

Help us to welcome the new ideas You are conceiving by Your Spirit. We surrender ourselves anew to You. Speak to our hearts and give us the wisdom to discern Your directions. Fill us with Your unselfish love, so that we will reach beyond ourselves to the opportunities You provide.

Without You, we can do nothing, O, Lord, so fill us with Yourself, and extend Yourself through us today. We praise You, most merciful and wise God. We humble ourselves before You and thank You for Your grace. Amen.

Chapter Five
A Pilgrim's Prayer

Jesus, what a wonderful feeling it is to call you "Lord." What a joy it is to know deep down in my heart that I may come anytime—day or night—to Your throne of grace and be received. I will not only be received, but I know that You throw open wide the door when You see me coming!

I have been created for praise and fellowship with You—to know You and to love You forever. I anticipate what You have in mind for my life! When I spend time with You daily, gratitude wells up in my heart, because I'm able to share myself openly with You. Thank You for prompting me to be totally honest with You, for in this honesty, I learn more about myself. When I am honest with You, You are better able to guide me by Your Spirit and free me from any bondages in my life.

Thank You for Your wisdom that You pour into my life, and for giving me understanding when I need it the most.

I look to You this day, heavenly Father, for strength and guidance. Without You, I can do nothing. You are my power, my strength, and my fortress. You keep me calm in the midst of storms and give me hope when life becomes overwhelming.

Thank You for "sticking closer than a brother" (Proverbs 18:24) and for giving me direction in the midst of the tumults of life. I thank You, Lord, for always being there for me. Strengthen me, and fortify my inner self so that I will reflect Your love again today. Thank You for loving me always. In Jesus' name. Amen.

The Christ

Whoever believes that Jesus is the Christ is born of God...By this we know that we love the children of God, when we love God and keep His commandments. (1 John 5:1–2)

Thank You, O, Lord, for the assurance that I am Your child! Your Word tells me that if I believe that Jesus is the Christ, then I have been born into Your kingdom. Lord, I believe that Jesus is Your only begotten Son. I believe You sent Him to save me from my sins. Jesus is my Deliverer, my King, my all in all. Thank you for wooing me until I accepted Jesus as Lord of my life, and the King of Kings and Lord of Lords! Jesus, become the leader in all of my life. I want no other guide.

Thank You, Lord, that the more I love You, the more I love others. This is how I am enabled to love other people: when I love You, Lord God, and do my best to obey You. In this obedience it's as if You are saying, "Friend, go up higher" (Luke 14:10b). Draw me close to You today and cause me to become more like You. This is a miraculous process, and I thank You for it.

Lord Jesus, thank You for coming to our world. Thank You for becoming the Deliverer and Savior, not just of the world, but also for me personally. Come into my heart anew this morning. Refresh me in my spirit. Fill me again, and I will follow Your direction, with Your joy, throughout my day! In Jesus' name. Amen.

How beautiful on the mountains are the feet of those who bring good news. —Isaiah 52:7 NIV

Victory That Overcomes

For this is the love of God, that we keep His commandments... For whatever is born of God overcomes the world. And this is the victory that has overcome the world—our faith. (1 John 5:3–4)

This morning Lord, I am reminded of Your power and how You control the universe. In the midst of turbulent times, I thank You for steadying my heart with Your peace. Though the strong winds may blow, You are with me. Even though I don't understand everything in Your plan, I trust You that You are in control and have my best interests in mind.

Thank You for Your Word which brings new life to me each day. Your Word tells me that if I love You, I will obey Your commandments. I do love You, Lord, and my heart's desire is to follow You. At times it seems difficult to hear and obey Your still, small voice. But each time I do obey, my love for You is deepened and my faith grows stronger.

Thank You for showing me the simplicity of obedience. Slowly I'm learning that obedience is required to become an overcomer in this life. You tell me that if I am born of God, I can overcome the world.

This is Your love: that I keep Your commandments. Remind me again and again of joys gained, faith increased, and abundant love experienced when I listen to and obey Your Word. Thank You for giving me the strength to be an overcomer in this world! In Jesus' name. Amen.

The Water, the Blood, and the Spirit

> *Who is he who overcomes the world, but he who believes that Jesus is the Son of God? This is He who came by water and blood—Jesus Christ; not only by water, but by water and blood. And it is the Spirit who bears witness, because the Spirit is truth. (1 John 5:5–6)*

*I*t is with a heart full of gratitude that I come to You, Lord God, thanking You for Your goodness. By Your Holy Spirit, You bear witness to my heart that Jesus has saved me and that I am an overcomer of the world!

How exciting this walk with You is! How exciting is the way You continue to instruct me as I walk closer and closer to You. Thank You, Lord, that even during those times when I do not understand Your ways, I can have the assurance that You are ever with me—teaching me, perfecting me, and showing me daily how important it is to be found in You, seeking Your face, and waiting upon Your Word. Thank You for the anticipation in my heart of good things to come, and thank You that hope continues to lead me on in the path You have chosen for me.

Father, You tell me that Jesus came by water and blood, and not water only. Thank You, Lord, that You help me to keep an open and searching mind and heart so that Your Spirit can whisper the words I need to hear! You have a perfect, unique pattern for each child of God; how special we all are to You!

Thank You, Lord Jesus, that You came to this earth to fulfill all righteousness. Thank You that because of Your obedience, all power was established in and through You in heaven and earth! Thank You for Your obedience in baptism, Your death on the cross, and for sending Your Holy Spirit to lead, comfort and guide us!

Cause me to be sensitive to the teaching of Your Spirit. Holy Spirit, whisper the words I need to hear this day. Cause me to mature in You so that my witness will be a shining light to others, and in so doing, I will please the Father. In Jesus' name. Amen.

God's Witness in the Earth

For there are three that bear witness in heaven: the Father, the Word, and the Holy Spirit; and these three are one. And there are three that bear witness on earth: the Spirit, the water, and the blood; and these three agree as one. (1 John 5:7–8)

*F*ather, I seek to feel Your presence today as I wait upon You. I know that You are always with me. Thank You for the arms of Jesus as He watches over me and holds me steady through storms in my life.

Thank You for the Trinity—Father, Son, and Holy Ghost. What a great mystery that is to our human minds. But I thank You that You are who You are and that You are a great and mighty God, one and yet three! Thank You for growing faith that confirms that truth.

Lord, Your Word tells me today that You bear witness in heaven as well as in the earth. Thank You for this, and for the Spirit who lives inside my heart and is my Comforter, Teacher, and Guide.

I recall the words spoken by the Father when the Spirit descended upon Jesus at His baptism, "This is My beloved Son, in whom I am well pleased" (Matt. 3:17). Thank You that we, too, are privileged to receive water baptism. Indeed, just as Your Word says, water bears witness on the earth!

I have been saved from sin! I am cleansed by the blood of the Lamb! I am united in fellowship with my Creator. Father God, what mercy, what compassion You have toward me! Thank You for Jesus' blood sacrifice. Thank You that Christians now have full access to Your throne room, and You bid us, "Come!" In Jesus' name. Amen!

God Is Trustworthy

> *If we receive the witness of men, the witness of God is greater; for this is the witness of God which He has testified of His Son. He who believes in the Son of God has the witness in himself; he who does not believe God has made Him a liar, because he has not believed the testimony that God has given of His Son.*
> *(1 John 5:9–10)*

Everywhere I look, O, Lord, there seems to be dishonesty, lying, cheating, half-truths, deceitfulness, and a lack of integrity. People who can be trusted are few and far between. I cling to You, O, Lord, for in a world of unfaithfulness, You are a faithful God! In these days of deceitfulness, help me to share the integrity of Your Word, which are unfailing promises available to those who would receive them. Only You are completely trustworthy.

When I search in other places for truth, I am often disappointed. Forgive me for such readiness to receive testimony from men when I know in my heart that Your testimony is greater. I praise You for Your promises in Your Word.

Now, Lord, help me be eager today to share that testimony with neighbors and friends who don't know You. Help me remember to let my witness be overflowing with Your love and compassion. In Jesus' name. Amen.

All Believers Have a Witness

And this is the testimony: that God has given us eternal life, and this life is in His Son. He who has the Son has life; he who does not have the Son of God does not have life. (1 John 5:11–12)

Father, You tell me plainly that if I believe Jesus is the Son of God, then I have Your witness within me. Help me to grow in stature until I am willing to share my testimony. Give me the boldness necessary to acknowledge You daily. I acknowledge that I serve a risen Savior, that He has taken up residence within me, and that I am in Him, and He is in me. He gives me the power to live a supernatural life through His grace and mercy.

Thank you for eternal life made possible through Jesus. Because we have Jesus, we have life; and those who do not have Jesus do not have life. You tell us in Your Word, "The harvest truly is plentiful, but the laborers are few" (Mt. 9:37). Help me to be a carrier of Your truth. Give me boldness to draw others to You.

Hear my prayer, O, Lord, and develop my witness until it brings glory to You! In Jesus' name. Amen.

How beautiful on the mountains are the feet of those who bring good news. —Isaiah 52:7 NIV

Knowing and Believing

*These things I have written to you who believe
in the name of the Son of God, that you may
know that you have eternal life, and that you
may continue to believe in the name of the Son
of God. (1 John 5:13)*

Lord, thank You for Your anointed Word which You
have inspired and preserved through the ages. Thank
You that Your words will stand forever. Father God, You
continue to teach with repetition the concepts I need
to hear over and over again. Repetition causes truth to
be absorbed in my spirit and Your teaching is new and
vibrant each day!

My main purpose in life is to know You. First John
has taught me that I might *know* that I have eternal life
if I *believe* on the name of the Son of God. Believing
and knowing can be two entirely different processes! I
believe Lord! I thank You that I can say with assurance,
"I know that I know that nothing or no one can change
my faith in God!" In Jesus' name. Amen.

God Hears Our Prayers

Now this is the confidence that we have in Him, that if we ask anything according to His will, He hears us. And if we know that He hears us, whatever we ask, we know that we have the petitions that we have asked of Him. (1 John 5:14–15)

Lord, how precious is the knowledge that I can greet You personally each day. How grateful I am that because of the shed blood of Jesus Christ, I am privileged to come into Your throne room at any time. What privileges I have as your child! Thank you for the exhilaration of knowing that You listen to our prayers and that You answer our petitions.

Your Word tells me to have confidence in You when asking anything according to Your will. Because I do my best to abide in You and allow Your words to abide in me, I thank You, Father, for the confidence I have in knowing that my prayers are heard!

Forgive me for the times I have failed You. Fill my heart with Your very self that I might walk in Your perfect will today. And, Father, when successes occur in my life through answered prayer, I will be careful to give You the praise! I love You, Lord, with all of my heart. Thank You for hearing my prayers. In Jesus' name. Amen.

Praying for Others

If anyone sees his brother sinning a sin which does not lead to death, he will ask, and He will give him life for those who commit sin not leading to death. There is sin leading to death. I do not say that he should pray about that. (1 John 5:16)

Father, thank You for Your precious love—Your love which covers a multitude of sins! I praise You for Your forgiveness that understands my weak nature, and yet continues to give pardon and acceptance.

You give the body of Christ the ministry of reconciliation. We are privileged to offer the world a measure of Your love, mercy, compassion, and grace. Help me to grow personally in this ministry of reconciliation. When I see my brothers and sisters in Christ sinning, give me an understanding heart on how to approach them.

Forgive me for standing back and judging instead of trying to help them overcome their sin. Help me refrain from procrastination and excuses, but instead cause me to care enough about the members of the body of Christ so that I see possibilities in situations, pray for errant persons, and do whatever is possible to help.

O, God, You whose mercy is from everlasting to everlasting, instill in me a measure of that mercy. Help me to care for brothers and sisters more today than I did yesterday. Help me to be quicker to forgive than to judge.

Your Word tells me that there is no sin too large for You to forgive except blasphemy against Your Holy Spirit. I intervene for Your children who are in sin. Forgive them, Father, according to Your lovingkindness. Bring them to repentance so that a right relationship with You may be restored. I pray this in the precious name of Jesus. Amen.

Becoming People of Righteousness

All unrighteousness is sin, and there is sin not leading to death. (1 John 5:17)

Lord God, You must yearn for a righteous people—a people who will trust You and follow You in any circumstances.

Forgive me for failing to recognize my shortcomings as sin, for You tell me that "all unrighteousness is sin." Thank You for telling me of Your love which forgives all sin.

Thank You for the strength and the power to refrain from sinning. Help me become so reliant upon You and Your Spirit's direction that I move farther away from bad habits and closer to righteousness and right living!

My prayer, Lord God, is that I will become more and more aware of sin in my life the way that You see it. I pray that I will stop making excuses for myself and others. I pray that I will walk so close to You that Your Holy Spirit will correct me immediately when temptation comes. Help me to recognize my sin as sin, and draw me into immediate repentance!

Thank You for Your forgiving love and abundant grace. Thank You that all things are possible through Jesus Christ. Help me to be a person of righteousness today. In Jesus' name. Amen.

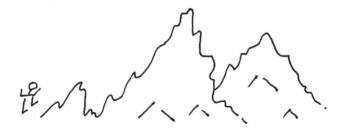

How beautiful on the mountains are the feet of those who bring good news. —Isaiah 52:7 NIV

Being Born of God

We know that whoever is born of God does not sin; but he who has been born of God keeps himself, and the wicked one does not touch him. (1 John 5:18)

Today is Your day, Lord God. You created it for Your glory, and I am so privileged to revel in Your presence. You give deepening observations about Your Word when I spend time with You. Life is exciting because You give me new life each day. Thank You for Your abiding presence within my heart which gives me confidence, purpose for living, and love for the body of Christ!

Lord God, in Your Word, You tell me those who are born again do not sin. Thank You for correcting me when I do sin. Thank You for helping me move away from any habits of sin, and help me to recognize that all unrighteousness is sin in Your eyes. Thank You for gentle quickening and conviction by Your Holy Spirit when I do sin, even when I commit what I would consider to be the smallest sin! You have given me the desire to move away from all unrighteousness.

Hold me securely to Yourself, Lord Jesus, and help me stand against temptation in Your precious name. I am grateful for the power and the right to use the name of Jesus to war against temptation. Increase my faith where I need it most, and forgive my unbelief. I pray in the precious name of Jesus. Amen.

Jesus—True God and Eternal Life

We know that we are of God, and the whole world lies under the sway of the wicked one. And we know that the Son of God has come and has given us an understanding, that we may know Him who is true; and we are in Him who is true, in His Son Jesus Christ. This is the true God and eternal life. Little children, keep yourselves from idols. Amen. (1 John 5:19–21)

Thank You, God, for the security of knowing that You hold me in the palm of Your hand and the evil one can have no part of me. Teach me to war against the forces of evil all around for I am able to recognize evil when I am walking in Your light. Keep me from living in pride, but give me Your wisdom to ward off evil influences all around.

Lord God, thank You that Your Son has come, and because He has come, I have understanding. You gave the world Him that is true, our Savior, Jesus Christ, and You give eternal life to those who trust in Jesus, for He is eternal life!

The world is full of enticements and temptations— so many attractive enticements which You call "idols" that can easily lure me from Your light to gradual darkness. Give me Your wisdom each day to discern the difference between Your path and the path which I should not follow. Lord, do not allow anything or anyone to replace You in my life. Have Your own way with me, Lord. Be my true leader and guide today, as I put my trust completely in You. In Jesus' name. Amen.

A Pilgrim's Prayer

Lord God, today is another day in my walk of salvation! How exciting to know that each day unfolds my life with You!

Give me attentive ears today to hear Your voice and a transparent heart that reveals everything to You. Thank You for knowing my heart, even before I tell you what I think or feel. Reveal to me my innermost motivations and desires, for I am sometimes at a loss to know them myself.

Father, there are mighty forces at work in our world—forces which I do not always understand, but You know everything from the beginning to the end. Show me Your way and Your will today so that I am able to contribute to the work of Your kingdom.

The only way our world can possibly be transformed is when we who are walking out this precious salvation with fear and trembling, accept the responsibility of bringing light to a confused world. Let those of us who believe, so let our light shine that hope, love, courage, and purpose are transferred to the discouraged, the lost, and those who are searching for meaning in a topsy-turvy, sin-ridden world! You've commissioned believers everywhere to do Your work. Help us all to be led and empowered daily by Your Holy Spirit as He will lead and guide us into all truth, just as Jesus promised.

Lord, renew spiritual vitality in the body of Christ! Strengthen the weak hands that hang down! Awaken our leadership! Arouse the sleepers! Help us confound the enemy! Thank You for giving us weapons that are powerful against the enemy. Arouse in all of us the courage of our convictions. Thrust us out into a world that needs the light of Your love!

Father, Your love can change the hardest of hearts. The power of Your love at work in believers can permeate situations that seem impossible to the natural mind. Let Your wonderful love flow out freely. Make a difference through me, for I want to bring the light of Your loving influence into the darkness. Thank You for this wonderful, powerful gift, which can help change the world! In Jesus' name. Amen.

Postscript from a Mountain Climber

*How beautiful on the mountains are
the feet of those who bring good news.*
—Isaiah 52:7 NIV

I am not satisfied with a mediocre Christian life,
are you? I believe God is telling us that there are mountains to climb, and spiritual dimensions to explore that
will give excitement and purpose to everything we do.
The Lord of life wants to add His vibrancy to all of our
days. There are roads to travel, valleys to walk through,
and summits to reach. And He wants to accompany us
daily on this pilgrimage! As we continue to pray and
stay close to Him, He will be with us every step of the
way.

Grace and Peace,
Mary Jane Fischer

*For you are a holy people to the Lord your God,
and the Lord has chosen you to be a people for
Himself, a special treasure above all the peoples
who are on the face of the earth. (Deut. 14:2)*

Postscript from the Holy Spirit

Today I am seeking mountain climbers to do the work of My Kingdom. Are you willing to be a mountain climber? Are you willing to scale the heights of my love for the sake of others?

Rest in my love. As you rest in My presence, I shall fill for service. The problem may lie in your resting…My children languish for a lack of rest. My rest is all encompassing. My rest comes from your willful act of laying down every burden, every desire, every goal, every notion, every physical need and coming to Me with single focus. What is that focus? Simply a desire to spend time with Me and Me alone. It means stopping your movement and willfully turning off every response to the demanding world. Are you ready to worship? Are you ready to praise Me? Are you ready to relax in my love?

Now think about Me. What have I done for you? Yes, verbalize your thoughts, for in this verbalization statements take on greater significance. In this verbalization My presence fills the moment. In this verbalization you will release greater emotion and praise in My behalf. Little children, now you are ready to praise Me. Now you are ready to anticipate My voice. Now you are ready to hear, and rejoice, and obey.

Mountain climbers do not become mountain climbers in an instant. Mountain climbers seek Me daily, wait upon me, and show much patience while I ready the heart for the work of My Kingdom. I fill you with My love. I fill you with My joy. I fill you with patience and the desire to acknowledge My every move in your life. Most of all, I fill you with the desire to show mercy to a world that is blind to My daily workings.

Now go to the hungry, go to the sinners, go to the indifferent, the blasphemers, the lost and the ones who insist on ridiculing the supernatural. You now go in My courage. My wisdom shall wind you through every intricate step of the day. Remember, I am with you always, even unto the ends of the earth! Scale the heights and depths of My love today as you dispense for My glory. Watch Me work through you because of your obedience…you are becoming my mountain climbers!

To order additional copies of

Praying Through First John

volume 1

Scale the Heights of God's Love!

Have your credit card ready and call

Toll free: (877) 421-READ (7323)

or send $8.95* each plus $4.95 S&H**

to
WinePress Publishing
PO Box 428
Enumclaw, WA 98022

*Washington residents please pay 8.4% tax.
**Add $1.00 S&H for each additional book ordered.

Author's address: 437 Park Rd., Mt. Carmel, IL 62863
Email: GeoMJ@wworld.com

Notes

Notes

Notes

Notes

Notes

Notes

Notes

Notes

Notes

Notes

Notes